PRAISE FOR THIS BOOK

I found myself sitting up straight with several bolts of insight reading *A Woman's Guide*. The combination of practical, real life examples you can easily comprehend along with fun exercises to stretch you into unfamiliar growth was powerful. Ann demonstrated a balanced masculine/feminine integration in how she tells this story, so it's a concrete example of what that looks and feels like. This guide is one that truly lives up to its name. As a much-read, occasionally jaded reader she electrified me with what was on offer. I highly recommend this as a big step forward from the usual 'self-help' manual. It's a living breathing expression of what is being taught and beyond the usual women's 'guidance'.

– **Lisa Greenfield,** *Truth in Hand*

What a relief it is reading a book that empowers women to find tools for love and partnership. Not only does Ann O'Brien's relationship expertise give us clear information, but she also does it in a playful, no-nonsense way. Ann's wisdom on healing the masculine and feminine within us creates space for deep healing that makes love more approachable for each of us. Thank you, Ann, for being the light that women need!

– **Marla Mervis-Hartmann,** *Creator of "Love Your Body Love Yourself"*

If you're like most women, you obsess over love — you get high when it's happening and over-analyze when things go South. This is not just a relationship book. *A Woman's Guide to Conscious Love* brings clarity to the things that trip us up in our relationships — from unhealthy family patterns to past lives, previous lovers to cultural programming.

Through keen wisdom, storytelling and humor, Ann O'Brien explains how energy gets stuck or misplaced; but more importantly, she gives you tools to clear it up for yourself, truly connect with your heart, and prepare to love and be loved in ways you only dreamed possible.

- **Stacy McCrory,** *Licensed Marriage & Family Therapist and Owner of TwoCan Retreats*

A Woman's Guide to Conscious Love adds a whole new dimension to therapy by addressing the energy we can't see. It's practical, non-judgmental and it makes complete sense of things most of us feel but can't pinpoint. Even better, it includes incredible resources and guided meditations to set yourself up for success. I'm impressed.

- **Rudi Lion,** *MFT*

A Woman's Guide to Conscious Love brilliantly empowers a woman to understand herself and how to truly love and appreciate her man. Ann´s way of teaching is non-judging and full of love, and will inspire any woman to a deeper path of loving herself and the masculine in the dance of love.

- **Karen Brody,** *Man Coach and author of Open Her, Activate 7 Masculine Powers to Arouse your Woman´s Love & Desire*

A WOMAN'S GUIDE TO
CONSCIOUS
LOVE

NAVIGATING THE PLAY OF
FEMININE AND MASCULINE ENERGY
IN YOUR RELATIONSHIPS

a post-feminist love manual by

ANN O'BRIEN

PUBLISHER'S NOTE

This book is intended to support you in your relationships and self-healing path. That said, the meditation techniques, exercises and suggestions offered in this book are not promised or intended to take the place of medical, psychological or other professional services. Where expert assistance is needed, one should enlist the help of a qualified professional.

.....

Book design by Lucinda Rae.

Name: Ann O'Brien, author.

Title: A Woman's Guide to Conscious Love: Navigating the Play of Feminine and Masculine Energy in Your Relationships

ISBN 978-1-7344128-1-9

To all those ready to live and love

as you have never done before.

TABLE OF CONTENTS

ACKNOWLEDGMENTS

To all my partners, love interests and friends who've made their way into this book... you know who you are. You've been my greatest teachers.

To my incredible clients who trust me with their most personal stories, hopes, and fears. I wouldn't see and know so much if you didn't show me.

To my intuitive and spiritual teachers- particularly Michael Tamura, Mary Bell Nyman, Hope Hewetson and the late John Fulton. To the many healers who've supported me, including Louise Swartswalter, Eileen Macfarlane, Julie E and Lauren Whittaker- for helping to keep my body and energy field clear and vibrant.

To my Aikido teachers and mentors- most notably Hiroshi Ikeda, Tres Hofmeister, Lee Lavi Ramirez, Mike Jones and Chris Bergerud. To my training partners and students, for all you have taught me about the energy exchange in relationship.

To my yoga teachers, for helping me relax, breathe, embody, soften into my feminine and find unity within- Max Strom, Annie Carpenter, Jason Frahm and more. To my African dance teachers who would wave goodbye saying, "Be juicy... go home happy!"

To Laura, Lisa, Zita, Bridget, Elysia, Franky and all my dear friends who've cheered me on, laughed with me at the little things, and given me late-night readings when I got stuck.

To Kat Tepelyan for your web and design brilliance, for making the complicated simple- and especially for "getting me" and supporting my success. To Forrest Podrat for creating beautiful images and for your loyalty.

To Karen Brody and to Ayn Cates Sullivan for going before me and sharing your wisdom on book-writing and publishing. Ayn, I remember I was drawn to talk with you back in 2010- when you brought my daughter's father to the raw foods retreat where we all met- and now I know why.

To Robin Quinn for your editing magic, for being the eyes that are not in my head. I appreciate your expertise, conscientiousness and enthusiasm. To Lucinda Rae for your gorgeous, intuitive cover and layout.

To my teachers and colleagues from Naropa University's writing program, and to all my singer-songwriter and poetry friends. Writing can be solitary, but our community back then made it into an exciting conversation that gave me fuel.

To my fellow leaders and pioneers working towards a new paradigm of conscious relationships and masculine-feminine dynamics on this earth. Clearly, we need you.

To everyone at True Nature Healing Arts... It's an honor to be part of this community of wise, like-minded and friendly souls. Your cold-brew coffee and beautiful, warm cafe sustained me through countless hours of writing.

To my grandparents, Nana and Papa, for showing me "Yes, Dear" done right. For my Nana's sweet feminine taking me into nature, and for Papa's head-butting that became "I'm so proud of you!" since he's gone to the other side. To my parents... for the gift of this life and for your generous, unconditional support.

To my daughter, the light of my life... for the honor of supporting your intuition and power in ways no one knew how to give me. You give me daily practice in supporting the empowered feminine, and I am confident you'll take this work to a whole new level, beyond anything I could imagine now.

INTRODUCTION

In recent news, women have been stepping up and accusing powerful men of sexual harassment. With the #MeToo movement on social media, all kinds of women are speaking up about this.

In my work as an intuitive healer and coach, the #1 topic I'm asked about is relationships. I am hearing two things really strongly:

1. Women want men, and they want their men to give them the best the masculine has to give. They want their men to ravish them, to inspire them, to be trustworthy, and to protect and provide.

2. Women complain a lot about men. They come to me when he disappears or doesn't follow through, when he's too domineering or critical or manipulative, when he's depressed and boring, when they stop having sex, when he doesn't have a job or money, when he starts looking for "Mommy," or when he goes out drinking or starts looking at other women.

Wanting a man and yet complaining about men is a recipe for disaster! The number of women who do it gives me a lot of business, but it's also shown me a great need for a book like this.

Our grandmothers' ("Yes, Dear") generation of women needed men for survival, and so they put up with a lot of crap in order to have it. They overlooked their own needs and men's flaws due to necessity. Men took on a more patriarchal role. This made things simpler in a sense.

Our mothers' feminism wouldn't have that. They required the freedom and respect our grandmothers gave up. The pendulum swung towards women pushing men away, getting angry and demanding the same rights. In this process women gained a degree of power but gave up much of their femininity. And some men got softer, giving up a level of their masculinity out of remorse for what the feminine had been through. Many men also feared losing women's love and respect, and so they put a damper on their own masculine edge.

Now everyone is confused. But it's a great time for recognizing the masculine and feminine parts of each of us, and it's also a powerful time for healing our true nature that got lost in re-evaluating our roles. Somehow, in reacting to wounds and emphasizing "appropriate behavior," we have forgotten our natural energy and limited our happiness—not only in relationships, but in life as a whole. Polarity and unity can co-exist, and this book is designed to show you how.

Women tell me they still desire the masculine. And when I work with men who are struggling, I see how relieved they are when I support their masculinity while allowing their vulnerability.

To see the true masculine and feminine, just look to nature. Vast open spaces, the force of the sun or the riverbanks are all masculine elements. The rushing waters, blustery winds, or the rage of fire are all part of the feminine—and so is the sweet singing of a bird, the moonlight and the fragrance of a flower. Mother Earth doesn't hold back. She expresses it all without sentiment.

When the feminine is not served or cannot express freely, she lets you know. Right now, our planet is in a critical state, and the masculine-feminine relationship is the biggest wound on the planet. And deep down, I think we all want to heal it.

MY STORY

Life often makes more sense in retrospect. Growing up, I felt other people's emotions as my own, which confused me. At the same time, I was pulsing with creativity and passion, and I struggled to find a place to put it. It seemed everyone around me had resigned themselves to numbness, and I questioned whether my energy was ok. I yearned for someone to inspire me, to truly meet me.

"Maybe if I hold back like everyone else, I'll be loved," I surmised unconsciously. For years, this decision directed my life as a "runaway healer," that is, I unknowingly suppressed myself and tried to make people around me feel better. And, of course, it didn't work. My abandoning myself only made me feel more lost, and it didn't give anyone else the opportunity to feel me and love me either.

When I was eight years old, I chased a boy on the school playground trying to kiss him, and he punched me in the stomach. I fell to the ground with the wind literally knocked out of me. For years, I went for passionate, dramatic love that always seemed to end up in a story of hold back - overextend - get rejected. Then I went for "pretty good" relationships that didn't trigger that story, and that allowed my relationships to last awhile.

In my early years, I healed my father. My mother would complain about his drinking and then ask me to talk with him. "Aw honey, you have a way with him," she'd say. I was confused because it felt like grown-up stuff, yet she acted as if it was my job. I did seem to be good at it. His drinking taught me a lot about spiritual energy because he would "come and go" from his body depending on whether he was drunk or sober. I longed to connect to a person whose body was right there but whom I couldn't feel consistently.

Our early challenges can show us our destiny. My problem was healing men, and it's also my gift. All my life, I've studied how to do it in empowering ways for all.

My mom was operating off of her own programs about how to be feminine (to her, feminine = helpless), and so I didn't respect her. I was aching for an example of feminine power.

Beginning at age 12, I studied psychic abilities, astrology, tarot, and Eastern religion and philosophy. In high school, the boys teased me, calling me a witch. I spent many high-school afternoons calculating astrology charts and studying relationship compatibility. I still have these books, most pages dog-eared and marked up with different color highlighters for the various boys I knew.

In my teens and early 20's, I had one steady boyfriend after another. I had no trouble attracting guys, though having the skills to choose well and keep things going was another story. After a difficult breakup with my college boyfriend, I then had about 10 years of being mostly single. This was hard, but in retrospect was an important period of self-discovery. I delved into my spiritual trainings and personal development in a way that might not have been possible in relationship. I explored my creativity and started my business, to the point where I had a solid foundation of self-love and inner security.

Life reflected this back to me by sending me a man who was ready, willing and able to commit. He showed up on time with flowers, a clean car and dinner reservations. Basically, he was a "salt of the earth" type of guy. Having this stability for the first time in my life, I realized I wanted a child, which he did not. And so, we parted ways.

I met my daughter's father about a year and a half later. While he matched the visions I'd had about my partner coming in, he wasn't really "my type." As we became friends, I started to get the message: "This is the one you're supposed to be with." He was hearing the same thing, and so we got together and quickly got pregnant. We lived as romantic partners and steeped ourselves in family life, until we reached a point where we were all thriving. At that point, he and I chose to live separately as friends, and are now harmoniously co-parenting. He is an amazing, conscious man who was a great spiritual match, and helped me learn much of what I share in this book. He was also the right person to have this child with, and I'm sure this is a big part of why we got together.

There is no right or wrong way to do relationship, and you are not "broken" if your life doesn't look like a Hollywood movie. That's not what this book is about. Since I've experienced being single, dating getting married and having a family—I can say that each has pros and cons. I wrote this book mostly "in-between relationships," and feeling very fulfilled. I recognize the value of the free time and emotional perspective this has afforded me. Life has its cycles- and, looking back, we get what we get for a reason.

Now, I feel a ripening of all I have learned from my life and my clients, and I look forward to my next adventures. I'm excited to feel a readiness for more people to step into the aliveness and love they are meant for.

And now it's your turn...

Part 1

LOVE IS EVERYWHERE

Part 1 – Introduction

I know well the intense desire to find a mate, or to solve what's not working with your partner. Just wait. Before we talk about these things, let's get your foundation straight.

Otherwise, you could find "the One," only to have it blow up in your face or cement into a life of compromise. You could extinguish that fire, only to find yourself sinking in the flood you thought would fix things.

This book is about a new way to love and be loved. It starts with annihilating your need because (1) Love is all around you, and (2) You are love.

You may have heard these things before, and you may or may not believe them. I'm about to give you tools to feel your way into living this way, to prepare you to love more fully with another.

This may stretch you. Imagine the relaxation and pleasure at the end of the stretch.

LIVING BREATHING LOVE

Are you looking for ecstasy in love? There is a "secret sauce." Without it, you may have lovers. You may get or stay married. Yet you won't get what you want. Not even close.

You may think the magic comes from *him*. You live for the moments your heart feels that "zing." As soon as you've had one small taste of it, look out! You spend your days yearning for more. Nothing is more important than this feeling.

This kind of magic blasts your walls down. All your switches turn on, your whole body wakes up and every cell starts tingling. Your heart feels like it is bursting open. You look around and colors are brighter, that song on the radio feels like it's just for you, and everything dissolves into this moment. Time stops and you're satisfied, completely present here and now, yet one with everything. You forget all distraction, all wanting beyond what you have. Though you may yearn to express this love more and more, you yearn from fullness rather than grasp from emptiness.

Love stops us in our tracks. As women, this is both our deepest desire and our deepest fear—to be taken beyond what we thought we were.

It's not always easy. If you've ever been pummeled by love, you know what I mean. Love won't stand for control, expectations, and effort. It demands surrender. And until you learn to do this, every man will disappoint you.

The problem is, as feeling-oriented women, and as modern women in the age of feminism, we have been taught to be strong in a way that stamps out our sensitivity. We have learned not to need, and to take care of ourselves. We may very well have "proof" that receiving is not safe, that it makes us too vulnerable. And so, we resist the surrender we most yearn for, partly because we have no healthy role models for how to do it.

Despite our resistance, love never lets up. When your comfort zone fails, you are forced to stretch. In painful moments, you open. When "safe" choices blow up in your face, you risk. And boom— you feel more alive; you experience everything you've been looking for.

Love wants to give you everything. It's larger than your mind can grasp, and it's bigger than any one person. When you get this, you get more than you ever expected. With practice, you can learn to choose this before it chooses you. This is the subtle difference between bliss and annihilation.

If lovers have disappointed you, you may be confused about opening up to someone. That's ok. This book will help you find your way. And for now, try this… Imagine going through your days making love with life itself. In the midst of your normal activities, do your best to relax into a sense of magic, feeling a higher power guiding and directing you. You could call this "God," "the Divine," "the Universe" or whatever works for you.

Practice trusting more. At each crossroads say, "Take me, lead me where I need to go!" Be the vessel for inspiration and see how full and awake you feel. See if you can find pleasure in living this way.

Love is all around us. Appreciation will reveal it. And to know it opens the door for a human lover.

Next, you'll find an exercise you can do to connect to Universal love, so you can feel it for yourself.

PRACTICE: *Breathing and Connecting with Love Itself*

• *Sit in a comfortable chair or sofa with your feet flat on the floor. Having your feet on the floor will help you to stay present in your body so you can receive more.*

• *Close your eyes and begin to notice your breath. Take a few breaths, as you just relax and observe.*

• *On your next inhale, push your belly out. Allow the breath to fill the belly, solar plexus area and heart. Pause briefly at the top of the inhale, then begin to exhale in reverse. Soften your heart and abdomen, pulling the belly in as you finish the exhale.*

• *For the first few breaths, you're probably thinking about the steps I just gave, and putting some effort in. But once you get it, see if you can soften and simply allow more breath in and out. The breath is already there, and you are just a vessel.*

• *Just like love, the air you rely on is unlimited, ever-present and all-giving. Notice this now.*

• *Imagine a stream of golden light pouring down from above you. As you receive this light, imagine filling up with love. Sit taller and reach up with the crown of your head to allow more in. Imagine this love-light pouring down and into you, cascading through your body, bathing you in warmth and clarity.*

• *The more you practice this, the stronger your connection will become. Sit here breathing as long as you'd like.*

LOVING YOURSELF

If you love yourself, it's safe to be vulnerable. Healthy boundaries become natural. Your self-love says, "No thank you" or "I'd love to!" before you have a chance to blink. You're protected with no need for walls, and your power to attract is phenomenal. When you're anchored in self-love, there's no limit to your surrender. Otherwise, your tendency to feel so deeply is a blessing and a curse.

When you bite into that chocolate cake, your mouth explodes with pleasure. Hearing your best friend say you're beautiful, you soften and glow. However, falling in love makes you lose yourself. Long-term partnership gets boring or makes you feel dead inside. You might find yourself fighting or taking on problems that aren't yours. How on earth do you find your own center, your own bliss?

We want love but sometimes unknowingly push it way. Have you ever frozen when an attractive man looks your way or when your partner tries to help you? "Uh-oh. What does he want?" you wonder. "Am I ok here?" And then, assuming he's a fairly sensitive guy, he feels your discomfort and pulls back. He stops giving to you and to women in general, and everyone suffers.

Without self-love, you can't tell where he's coming from. Your stories that say, "I'm ugly," "I don't deserve," or "I can't trust" get mixed up with his gestures. They form filters that your subconscious *thinks* will protect you. Instead, the filters make it hard for you to feel the truth, causing you to brace yourself further. In the unlikely event he's even still trying, you can't feel anything good that he's giving you, and he cannot feel you. Connection stops. The stories win and they grow.

From self-love, you can easily sense if a man's energy feels natural and respectful. If not, you'll simply be able to brush off any manipulation because it won't "match" where you're at. On the other hand, if his actions feel authentic, your self-appreciation expands. He feels good too, as you receive him.

Every relationship is a mirror of something inside you. So, self-love is very helpful if you want to attract love from another. If men tend to treat you poorly, you know that self-love is probably something to work on.

Vulnerability is not the problem. Your vulnerability is a beautiful thing, *as long as you choose what to receive.* Self-love will show you what to choose.

DISCOVERING YOUR VALUE
THROUGH GIVING

"All that sounds good," you might say, "but *how* do I begin to love myself?" The first step is to simply *be* with yourself. Create space to feel your feelings and explore your own energy. Stop stuffing things and stop distracting yourself constantly. As we continue, I'll share meditations, writing exercises, and other practices to assist you.

Experiencing love beyond yourself involves getting in touch with something bigger. What makes you feel expanded? Is it going into nature—perhaps to the beach, forest or desert? Is it yoga or meditation or dancing? Do you like listening to music or watching movies?

One of my favorite ways to remember the love within me is to share my gifts with others. I've had days when I wanted to crawl in a hole, but then taught a class or helped a client and afterwards felt on top of the world. It's funny how that works. We all have something to give, and if you're not sure what you have, consider what you love to do naturally. Ask your friends how you support them or what they like best about you.

It's important to go inward and heal yourself, as well as give something of service to others. When you're giving, you can be as sensitive as you want; your giving protects you. This is a big relationship secret that we'll get into as we go.

YOU ARE ALWAYS "IN RELATIONSHIP"

I can see her face now. It was as if the sides of her lips were etched down in a permanent frown. "I don't have a relationship," my client claimed. "I don't even have family, no friends, no one I could call if I needed someone."

I was sitting across from her, fully present, just the client and me in the room. However, I couldn't feel her. I only felt her guard.

Now I get it. Years of disappointment have a way of making us bitter. However, what she wasn't seeing was how she created her experience.

We cannot function in the world and avoid relationships. They are everywhere. And in this case, I wasn't the clerk at the grocery store or a stranger on the street. I was someone she *paid* and took the time and energy to come see. I was there just for her, and still—she couldn't "have" me. It's not that relationships didn't exist in her life. It's that she wasn't receiving what she already had.

If you think about it... if you give someone a compliment or gift and they toss it away, disinterested or even disgruntled, you probably won't give them more. The Universe is like this. When loving, well-meaning people take an interest in you and you dismiss them, you send a message that says, "Leave me alone." Just a frown on your face will push people away.

I'm not saying to pretend to be always happy or to open your arms to everyone who looks your way. But you can be gracious. Saying something like "Thanks for checking in. I'm doing ok," or simply making eye contact and nodding will acknowledge the care coming your way.

I remember once being at the grocery store with a long-distance boyfriend. He wasn't committing, and he was encouraging me to find someone local. "Ann... Ann! You're missing all these guys," he urged me.

"Huh?" I looked up from my grocery list. He was totally right. There were several good-looking guys nearby. I'd been so focused on thinking *he'd* be my guy that I'd cut myself off from the options right in front of my face.

If you're looking for that special someone, or desiring more attention from the partner you have, one magic ticket is to receive love from anywhere and everywhere. Enjoy your friends and community, feeling how your heart opens as you do. That open heart is like a magnet that draws more love your way. It expands in you like a spiral, and your life becomes a dynamic exchange of giving and receiving. This energy is super attractive to a lover.

ATTRACTING WITHOUT NAMING

We make it so hard for the Universe sometimes. We get so narrow in our focus that we miss everything else it's trying to give us. This was me in the grocery store with my long-distance non-boyfriend.

You may have learned to be specific when it comes to manifesting. Ask and you shall receive, right? I've talked with women who have a list a mile long: "He's got to be tall, athletic, drive a nice car, make over $100K a year, live in X neighborhood, like the same movies and music I like, want to go to Italy, etc., etc." Even if you have a partner, you may have a list of all you want him to become and all you'd like to experience with him.

There are several problems with this type of list:

1. The more specific you get, the more you limit the Universe's (and other people's) ability to fulfill you.

2. It's all external. It doesn't even address what you *really* want! Not that your desires are bad, it's just more powerful to look at what's underneath them. Why do you want him to be tall? So you feel protected? To experience his power? Because that gives you the *zing* of great chemistry? Then ask for the feeling you desire, not the specific trait you think will get you that.

3. We need emotional power in order to manifest! You can ask for all the specifics in the world. However, if there's no feeling behind it, there's no fuel drawing him towards you.

Some women are so proud of their lists. I have been one of them. After all, it takes a certain level of clarity and self-love to get specific about the relationship you want. Bravo!

Now go deeper. What are you currently calling into your life? Don't worry about what it looks like. How does it *feel*?

Imagine melting as he kisses you. See the look in his eyes, feel the rush in your body. Anchor into the comfort you feel in his arms, awaken to the expansion he gives your life, visualize all the happy moments you share.

Can you do this without putting a face to it? I know, you may have someone in mind. A current love or past partner may have shown you what it's like to feel all this. You may want it with your current partner. That's ok. *Broaden* your vision. Beyond any person or idea you have now, there are hazy shapes. Give love a reference point, and then open to a sense of wonder.

The Universe won't let you down. Your feelings are fuel. Trust this.

PRACTICE: What Are You Attracting?

This is a practice to kindle your fires of attraction.

• For the following writing practice, use the form on the next page or create two columns—left and right—on a notepad or page of your journal. I highly recommend writing by hand rather than typing, as studies show that writing by hand is much more impactful on the subconscious.

• On the left side, write your list of everything you want. Don't try to be "evolved" just yet. Just note all the external things you'd like in a partner or relationship. Use my example above at the beginning of "Attracting without Naming," if it's helpful.

• Once you have your list, switch to the right side. Next to each "want," write how it will feel once you have it. For instance, if "tall" is on your list, you might say, "I feel protected," "I love having a powerful partner," or "I am in awe of him... this chemistry is amazing!"

• From this point on, when you think about your desires in love, just visualize yourself feeling all these great feelings. As you talk to your friends, as you daydream or meditate about your ideal relationship, stop worrying about the details. Life is unceasingly generous and infinitely creative. Enjoy, and open to having even more than you imagined.

What You Want	*How it Feels*

WHAT TRUE LOVE REQUIRES

"Really? This one?" my friend asked the Universe, looking at the older businessman who was her roommate. She'd been living with his wife, who was now working in Europe, and their teenage daughter. He'd been living separately, until their daughter needed a parent around, and so he moved in with my friend and his child.

They spent many hours sharing late-night meals, getting to know each other. She'd been pretty down on men at that time in her life, and he was far from her idea of a perfect match. But after about six months, my friend admitted to her roommate that she really had feelings for him.

"It's about time," he said.

Still, she was determined that nothing would happen until he worked things out with his wife, and so my friend left for the summer. As it turns out, it took quite a while for him to complete his marriage. But they knew, and eventually the two moved in together and married. Now, it's been twenty years and their relationship has been loving and harmonious.

It just goes to show that the Universe is always working in our favor. My friend wasn't even interested in dating at that time! He didn't seem like a viable option when he moved in. And yet circumstances created their courtship in a way that normal "dating" couldn't touch!

True love can be messy. It's perfect in its imperfection. It's rarely comfortable at first because comfortable doesn't get us where we want to go. This is where intuition comes in, bringing faith in the face of fear.

I'm not advocating chasing married men or avoiding dates. It's just that I've heard too many of these stories to not share at least one! Listen to your heart and listen to the signs. Be open because the love you seek IS around. You don't have to try so hard.

The evolution that love requires doesn't end once you have a lover. It especially doesn't end once you get married. We often think we've "arrived" once we get the guy or the ring. Actually, that's when the next chapter begins. Relationships will continually stretch us because we're all here to grow. Being willing to do this is one key to creating deep, harmonious, and lasting love. Otherwise, we either fight or compromise, which is why most relationships cause stress. Inspired love with another human is not always easy but in it we feel alive and it feels *right*.

PRACTICE: *Your "Thank-You" Letter to the Universe*

No matter what you've been through or are currently going through, there is a greater purpose. By finding gratitude, you'll step into a higher perspective that feels better! It may be like finding that tiny flower growing through cracks in the sidewalk. Even so, it's worth finding. You'll let go where you need to, and you'll attract more goodness your way.

Write a "thank-you" letter to the Universe. Say thank you for anything and everything you can think of-- your life as a whole, yourself, and all your relationships. Include your past or current partners—what's your favorite thing about each one? Consider including the lessons you learned through the hard times. What were the gifts that came with your challenges?

Your "Thank You" Letter

Part 2

MAKING SENSITIVITY
YOUR FRIEND

Part 2 – Introduction

The expansiveness of true love can be frightening. It sounds so beautiful and feels so good but then there's "reality."

Perhaps past trauma built walls around you. You don't want to repeat the pain of getting hurt or of risking and failing. Just feeling so much can make everyday life—let alone romantic relationships— overwhelming. Your walls have stories carved on them, that— consciously or not— lovers read and repeat.

Do you know your worth? Do you love yourself fully, on your good days and bad? To do so will help your love life immensely, and we'll talk about that in Part 2.

As a woman, your sensitivity is your strength. It not only makes life more enjoyable; it actually protects you. This is counterintuitive yet you'll trust it more the more you practice.

If you haven't honed these muscles, there are exercises to help you do so. I'll share some with you in the pages to come.

CREATING HEALTHY BOUNDARIES

Not only are your feelings the key to attracting your desires, they also protect you better than anything. Rules, walls, or the best techniques do nothing compared to your feelings! Your feelings know best what's right for you, and they'll lead you in the direction you need to go, moment to moment. Your instinctive "yes" or "no" is soft, appealing, yet indomitable.

Whether you're "in a relationship" or not, boundaries are important. Creating firm boundaries is a more masculine way. Most of us have learned this and may feel safe with it. There is a place for it, yet your stiffness also limits how much you can feel. It's possible to become too rigid and attract what you resist. It's even more possible that you abandon your femininity in enforcing this firmness.

Holding back and hiding your light is another option—but a less empowered one. It comes from an old paradigm saying the feminine is helpless, that vulnerability is unsafe. It comes from a fear of the feminine power. But if we are this powerful, shouldn't we be able to protect ourselves?

Besides feeling your feelings and your instinctive "yes" and "no" in the moment, it helps to get clear on your bottom-line requirements in relationship. Doing this helps with both attraction and boundary-setting.

Let's face it, relationships bring up lots of emotions! In the midst of these emotions, it can be hard to judge when to say "yes" or "no," or what to say or do.

Having your requirements in hand will always bring you back to earth and remind you what you stand for. Meanwhile, they tell the Universe what to send your way!

Next up is an exercise for getting clear on your requirements in relationship. This will establish your self-loving boundaries.

PRACTICE: What Are Your Requirements in Relationship?

Take out a pen and go back to your list of "wants" and resulting feelings from the "What Are You Attracting" practice in Part 1.

I'm going to ask you to create a new list, considering...

Which of the wants and feelings on this list are "must haves"? Using the following page or your journal, note those requirements on your new list. Add things if you'd like now. For example, you may need monogamy, mutual respect, or that your partner has a job and can support himself. Whatever you designate here is non-negotiable. Keep this list nearby. It will keep your head on straight when passion or another person's influence wants to lead you off course!

Beyond your "musts," everything else on your "wants" list is negotiable. Often the Universe gives us everything we ask for and more. However, there are times we think we want something and there's actually a better plan for us. So, it's important to have this wiggle room. Trust what comes and, at the same time, dream!

Your Non-Negotiable Relationship Requirements

COMING HOME TO YOUR BODY

One of my spiritual teachers, Michael Tamura, used to joke with us in workshops. He'd say, "Ask and you shall receive. But if you're not home to receive, UPS delivers next door."

When our sister, friend, or co-worker gets the guy, we cry and scream, "Huh? But what about ME?!" Sometimes we secretly scream at God because we think we're more attractive or more qualified. Or we go down the spiral of self-hate, self-doubt. We look at our butts or bellies in the mirror and wish we could shrink them. We beat ourselves up over something we said or did, wondering which little mistake we made to mess it all up.

Often, it's none of these things. Love sometimes goes "next door" when we're not present. When we're looking at our grocery list instead of around us. When we're holding back or hiding out, trying to stay "safe." When we're lost in a fantasy.

If you've had trauma, coming home to your body can feel scary, even life-threatening. If this sounds familiar to you, breathe and take a break whenever one is needed. Then come back to the exercises and ideas in this book.

Why is presence important and how do you get there?

I once attended a relationship workshop where a presenter shared the top traits men look for in women, based on a survey. While we might think men look for perfect boobs and butts, the top two answers were actually *confidence* and *sensuality*.

Think about it. A confident, sensual woman is *in her body*. She glows. A masculine man gets enlivened by her strength, wanting to match her, wanting to impress her further. He feels safe because he knows where she is and what she feels. This gives him trust in his own feelings. And he wants to dive in and get sensual with her!

By contrast, you've probably seen those women who are

completely "put together" but seem uncomfortable in their own skin. They're scattered, their words feel disconnected, and (despite the perfect makeup) there's a vacancy in their eyes.

Now, makeup can be a way of appreciating your body! But if you had to choose between getting enough sleep, meditating, eating well, exercising, and putting on makeup—I'd suggest putting on makeup last. Because you, the spirit, is the brightest light your body will ever hold.

Getting present is a process. It's a journey of gentleness, step by step. It may feel unfamiliar, excruciatingly uncomfortable, or plain boring.

Do your best to start with one simple act of self-care. Love yourself, even in little ways as you work up to the bigger ways. So what if you hate your stomach or butt? Don't try to stop all the negative thoughts. Just add in some loving ones.

There's one exercise I do with my five-year-old daughter before bed. We'll say, "I love you, toes; I love you, feet; I love you, knees…" all the way up to the top of her head. Having the physical reference of the different body parts helps these statements "land" in the subconscious.

Breathing, getting out in nature, and observing little details in your environment are good ways to get present. So is noticing the sensations in your body. For example, if you feel sad, ask yourself where the sadness is in your body. Let yourself imagine it even if you think you don't "know." Fake it til you make it! Is the sadness hot or cold, prickly or smooth? What color is it? What are its qualities? This type of body-awareness will come in handy later as you're communicating with a partner or love interest!

Being present in your body makes you more magnetic, more powerful, and much safer. Because not only are you available to receive your desires, there's no room for anything unloving to come in. That space is already taken. It's taken by *you*.

PRACTICE: Grounding and Replenishing

• *Sit in your comfortable meditation space, close your eyes, and say "hello" to your body and breath. Feel your feet on the floor and feel your bottom pressing into the chair.*

• *Now, imagine a giant tree trunk growing down from your hips and deep into the center of the earth. Pick your favorite tree, perhaps a redwood, oak, or cypress. This tree trunk is your "grounding cord." Exhale, and as you do, allow any energy that you don't need to now release down the tree trunk.*

• *You might be letting go of stress, unhelpful beliefs, other people's emotions, or old trauma. Don't worry about figuring it out. Just decide to let it fall away, down into the center of the earth.*

• *Once you create your grounding cord, you'll continue to release "excess" energy down it, and the cord will continue to "anchor" you to earth. You don't have to keep focusing on it. I usually check mine once a day, or as needed.*

• *When you feel complete with releasing, there is one more step to coming home to your body—replenishing! To do this, stay in meditation for a few more minutes with your eyes closed.*

• *Imagine a giant golden sun several feet above your head. This sun is a symbol of your own light. Put a magnet in the middle of the sun and allow it to draw your energy and power back from other people and places, the future and past. In your mind's eye, "see" streams of gold coming into the sun from anywhere and everywhere you left a part of yourself. Again, you don't have to "know" where it's coming back from. Just decide and imagine it.*

• *When the sun feels full and this process feels complete, picture all the light pouring into your body. From head to toe, from every cell to the edges of your skin, receive this gold. Start to glow, sparkle, and overflow with your own love and radiance.*

CLAIMING YOUR ENERGETIC SPACE

"You" consist of more than your body. This is why, if someone stands a foot away from you, you feel each other's energy.

We each have an aura, or electromagnetic field that extends approximately 2 to 3 feet around the physical body. Your aura holds emotions, thoughts, and energy. And just like the body, if it's not full of your own energy, it will fill up with energy from other people and your environment.

Every day, I re-claim my aura. Just like my body, I clear it out and I replenish my aura with energy that feels good to me. I'm going to share with you how to do this now.

PRACTICE: Balancing Your Energy Field

• *Sit in meditation, breathe and ground. Use the belly-diaphragm-heart breath and tree trunk image we have used previously. Sit tall and imagine golden light pouring into the crown of your head.*

• *With your eyes closed, "see" a bubble of light around your body. If you feel like you're just making this up, that's fine. How far out from your body is this bubble? Is it a foot? 3 feet? 6 feet? Or does it vary in size—perhaps bigger in the front and smaller in the back, or mostly even with little "dents" throughout? There is no right or wrong, so just let yourself imagine yours. What color or colors is this bubble?*

• *Once you get a sense of your energy bubble, also known as your aura, it's time to set it up the way you'd like it. First, ask yourself if you like the colors you see. Do they feel like you? Are they bright and clear, or dull and murky?*

• *A general rule of thumb is that dull, murky energy is either someone else's energy, or your own energy that's gotten stuck. As you fill up with color(s) that you love, any stuck or foreign energy has to leave. You could bring in pink for love or purple for spirituality or blue for peace. You may have a color pop up that just feels good! Imagine that color(s) filling up your bubble now. Have fun with it; there are many meanings to each color.*

• *From here, you'll want to balance out your energy field. Go ahead and smooth out your bubble, then imagine that it's 2 to 3 feet out around your body on all sides. See it above your head, below your feet, in front and back, left and right. Tuck it into your grounding cord under your feet. As you do, your aura starts to release energy just like your body has been doing.*

• *When you're done, fill in with a gold sun as you did previously. Call your light back from other people and places, future and past, and let that light pour into your body and aura to replace what you just released.*

Part 3

WHAT IS THE TRUE FEMININE?

Part 3 – Introduction

In the next two sections, we'll dive into the natural qualities of the feminine and masculine.

This is not about traditional gender roles. And yet, we'll look beyond the recently popular tendency to neutralize gender in attempt to heal the painful way men's and women's roles have been distorted.

The truth is, there ARE masculine and feminine energies in nature. You have all of these possibilities in you, in various proportions that change moment to moment. And you likely have a certain essence that's dominant in your love life.

If you think about a time when overwhelming waves of love melted you open, you may remember a tension beforehand. Perhaps it was the intensity of a fight, a breakup, or giving up that preceded love's arrival. Unity means so much more when there is first polarity. Then there is something to unify.

Nature is dynamic, not static. And so, denying the feminine and masculine denies reality, it denies life force, and I see people suffer for it.

So, let's take a look. What follows are some ways to recognize feminine energy...

INTUITION

My teacher said, "You women were born with intuition. I had to work for years to develop it." He had directed a highly regarded psychic school, so this was a big statement.

Probably because our bodies are designed to create and care for babies, we women need intuition. Pregnant woman and mothers are instinctively guided to choose the right foods and environments, and to feel into their children's needs to keep them safe and happy.

Even if we are not mothers, because of our receptivity, we need intuition to determine when to open, who to open to, and what to let in. Our feeling nature is highly developed.

Science will tell you that the hemispheres of our brain are actually different than men's. Our logical left brains naturally communicate with our creative and intuitive right brains. Not so with men! They tend to compartmentalize. And so, a woman's intuition is more easily accessed all the time.

RADIANCE

When we feel alive with love, we glow. The more we can steep ourselves in love itself, the more our radiance will expand exponentially.

Our light inspires men, women, and children. The world worships it, as evidenced by all the billboards depicting beautiful women. It's priceless and yet it's free.

Our light is like sunlight, moonlight, starlight. The feminine is like a rainbow of delight. There's something so magical about it. It is what we create from, since it is evidence of our love, our greatest feeling-fuel. We can give the world a glimpse of it as it dances around us, completely ours and never depleted, yet freely given for all to see.

FLUIDITY

The feminine is like the weather. Because we are feeling-oriented more than goal-oriented, we women change our minds and our moods like we change outfits. We might have a plan, but if it doesn't feel good in the moment, we naturally move in another direction.

Caring for children requires this of us, and whether we have them or not, we are biologically wired to "flow." If due to our work or other factors, we spend a lot of time in a masculine role, we may find it difficult to "flow." Like many things feminine, it doesn't feel as "safe" in our culture. However, flow is part of our feminine essence.

Sometimes we judge our flow. "I'm supposed to be doing something else right now," we think. Does this sound familiar? We can be so hard on ourselves! For example, I set a schedule for the writing of this book—Monday, Wednesday, and Friday. Do you think I wrote every Monday, Wednesday, and Friday? Of course not!

Some weeks I was busy with family or tasks and I couldn't find the space. Other times, I was having my own tantrums, meditation binges, and generally learning firsthand many of the things I've written about. Then the waters would calm, the stars would align, and I'd find myself waking up with whole chapters written in my head.

Structure is a good thing. As I'll discuss in Part 5, my schedule was one way of calling on my inner masculine in support of my feminine creativity. Without my Monday-Wednesday-Friday commitment, I might have let the "flow" of other people and life's demands pull me from my book much more than it did. On the days I did write, I was in heaven, so grateful to have the space and time set aside for my creativity.

ENERGY

Behind our radiance—fundamental to our fluidity—is raw energy. As the masculine protects, guides, and supports the feminine, we are the ones doing most of the moving! Though it sometimes appears he "directs" us, don't underestimate how much our energy influences his direction. Both roles are equally powerful, yet different.

Our energy wakes him up. His practice is presence, which is downright boring if there's nothing to be present to! Our energy tests him as much as it enlivens him.

The feminine is the "stuff" of life. Just as each flower, plant, and animal is unique, the Divine Feminine shows herself in infinite ways. The infinite palate of colors, sounds, and elements provide energy which can take various shapes.

Energy in and of itself is innocent. Mother Nature is unsentimental, totally honest. She will express depending on what she receives. The feminine is like this. The one given is that her energy *will* express.

PRACTICE: *Go into Nature and Observe the Feminine*

Go into nature. If you're in a city, do your best to get to a park or go out of town for a day or weekend. Put your phone away and get quiet. Observe rivers and oceans, the stars and the rains and the wind. Watch the spontaneity of animals. Notice the daily and seasonal changes in plants, the earth, the sun and moon and stars. When you're done, write down what you sensed.

Notes

UNCONDITIONAL LOVE

A mother's love knows no bounds. All of us women, mothers or not, are wired this way. We thrive on love. We feel secure when we feel connected in our loving relationships.

This is why most of my female clients come to me with love questions. This is what we fixate on. It's as if we can't focus on work, money, or anything else if we have a crush, a new relationship, or a relationship challenge.

This is also why many women stay in toxic relationships or relationships that no longer serve them. When it comes to love, we would rather have "something" than "nothing," even if that "something" is hurting us.

It's also why we women can take a stand for our partner's best selves. Our unconditional love is actually what calls them out on their bullshit; it is what stands by their side for years as they get a degree or build their business. It's the part of us that nurtures and gives, day after day, year after year.

CREATIVITY

Our feminine creativity is immense! Think about it… if you can make a new life with your body, what else can you make?

This energy in us is non-stop—before, during, and after our child-bearing years. Because of this wiring, we are more complex than men.

It is essential for women to continuously create. When not baby-making, we can express ourselves through work, fine arts, or practical creative tasks. If we neglect this part of ourselves or allow it to get suppressed, we easily get sick or depressed. If we aren't conscious of this part of ourselves, it may express through micromanaging our lives or other people, frivolous talking, or over-focus on problems.

So, I highly recommend celebrating your feminine creative energy and choosing your favorite positive outlets for it!

PRACTICE: *Choose Your Creative Outlets*

• *Sit in meditation, ground, and breathe. Close your eyes and imagine a gauge out in front of you. See that it has a dial or digital display from 0 to 100%. Then ask yourself, what percent of my feminine creativity am I currently able to access? In your mind's eye, "imagine" the number that shows up on the gauge. This will give you a clear idea of how much this aspect of you is shut down, if at all.*

• *Grab a pen. Use the space provided on the next page or pull out a pad of paper or journal. Answer the following questions.*

• *How DO you use your female creative energy now? List the positive and not-so-positive ways.*

• *How would you LIKE to express your creativity? List all the ways you can think of that would be do-able and healthy for you at this time.*

Notes

PRACTICALITY

If the masculine is the sky, the feminine is the ground under our feet. His ideas are vast. And yet we ask, "Is it done? Is it real?"

We say things like: "So you had a great meeting today? Tell me later; the baby needs changed..." "That's great that you're getting a promotion. Why haven't the bills been paid?" "You won your golf game? Please just come home and hold me."

He loves to get somewhere, to feel successful, to lead with his thoughts. You love to feel good and secure in your body, in tangible ways. All men and women have both sides. But it's often us reminding them, "Come down to earth!"

We can do this with a roar or with a smile. At different times, one or the other may be needed. This is a gift we have. Don't make him wrong for his ways; instead, gently nudge him into awareness of practical life. With a secret smirk in your heart, let him be your hero in his ability to bring heaven to earth.

STRENGTH

Most men gasp at a woman's ability to labor for hours, to withstand the pain of birth. We are built for this, and to care for our children non-stop, day after day, year after year.

Besides our biological wiring for baby-making, I sense it is our gentleness that allows us so much strength. Unless forced or forcing ourselves into ultra-masculine mode, we are not as driven towards "conquest" or "achieving." Unfortunately, many women still live that way, as evidenced by the epidemic of adrenal burnout. However, it is not our feminine essence.

In the *Tao Te Ching*, there is a passage {78}:

"Nothing in the world
is as soft and yielding as water.
Yet for dissolving the hard and inflexible,
nothing can surpass it.

The soft overcomes the hard;
the gentle overcomes the rigid."

(Lao Tzu's *Tao Te Ching* translated by
Stephen Mitchell, 1988.)

If you've ever tried to knock down someone who is stiff, you know what I mean. They are the easiest people to push over! By contrast, someone relaxed and centered will "hold their ground" much longer and require much more focus on your part to influence.

This is true not just physically but in all life. Someone rigid in their thoughts rarely wins an argument. A person unwilling to feel all their feelings, or empathize with others, gets stuck really easily.

Flexibility and softness bring endurance. This makes it easy to influence most anything.

RECEIVING

To be feminine is to be receptive. This is what allows us to feel pleasure, to receive a child or creative idea, to bring anything good into our lives. Done right, it is our greatest source of power.

Without discernment, it's not safe to receive and be vulnerable. I understand why so many women (and men) avoid it. If we haven't clarified our values, if we aren't comfortable in our bodies, if we don't know how to clear and replenish our energy fields—our receptivity tends to attract toxic energy, people, and situations.

In the martial art of Aikido, we practice receiving as much as we learn attacking. Learning this discipline, and particularly how receiving is a choice, has been a huge piece of my empowerment. We don't focus so much on fighting—or even defending—as we aim to harmonize with the energy coming our way. And so, we utilize a lot of beautiful dance-like moves and falls.

I will never forget being thrown by one of my early Aikido teachers. Then a 5th degree black belt, he knew me and could feel exactly how hard to throw me. The moment was right, and I flew down and back up in complete exhilaration. "Do it again!" I thought. Of course, the moment had passed. But I was blown away by feeling the dance of our energies. It wasn't just him—it was also my years of training that gave me the capacity to receive so much, so gracefully.

This type of dynamic play is the reward when you learn to receive AND have a partner you trust. This is why, in life, it's super important to choose wisely. At his best, the masculine has the capacity to hold all that you are. Your natural feminine is to keep moving—responding to and expressing all you feel, moment to moment, in appropriate ways. Knowing that your mind is there if you need it, you let your heart lead the way.

PLEASURE

Pleasure feeds the feminine. When we stop allowing ourselves pleasure or when we feel shame about it, it's like putting out our feminine light.

Busy with all of our responsibilities, it's easy for days, weeks, or even years to go by without pleasure. "Oh that? I'll get to it," we think, and it never seems to happen. From a night out with girlfriends to sex with our partners to a spa vacation, it never seems as practical as paying bills and doing dishes and taking care of everyone. We're too tired. It costs too much. Really?

There are little ways to find pleasure in everyday life. Buy or pick yourself some flowers. Give yourself a foot rub, or trade this with a partner. Put on your favorite song and circle your hips as you brush your teeth. Keep a delicious essential oil in your purse and take a whiff or put a dab on your wrists before a business meeting.

The real reason we don't have more pleasure in our lives as women is not because these things are hard, expensive, or time-consuming. It's because a woman in her pleasure is unstoppable. Her powers of attraction and creation are infinite. And our culture is scared of that, even as we revere it.

Be a revolutionary. Be a teacher. Gift the world by choosing pleasure and letting it nurture you. Be relaxed in a stressed-out world. Let your sparks light up other lights.

FEMININE ARCHETYPES AND CYCLES

Our lives as women have phases and the feminine has many aspects. Archetypically, we begin as the maiden—typically, a young, unmarried women. From there, most of us become mothers. Moving into our older years, we are crones, wise women filled with magic.

There are many variations on these archetypes. Another popular one labels women as either virgin, mother, or whore. While on some level we can transcend these categories once we're living whole, conscious lives (perhaps that's why there are so many archetypes these days!), they are real and helpful to understand.

For example, if you "mother" your man too much, he might not want to have sex with you. Or he might feel less of a man around you, so hold back from commitment. He may not fully understand this, but his primal self does. It can hurt because you're just trying to love and care for him, and you can't fathom why he pulls away. You try to love him more and it only makes it worse.

On the other hand, if he sees you as a whore, he'll want sex, but he probably won't marry you! Ouch! What's a conscious, multi-faceted woman to do?

The truth is, you have all these parts within you. You can't hide it. It's why he loves you and it's also why you intimidate him.

It's an art as a woman to dance from one role to the next, expertly knowing when to be your inner mother, crone, or whore. When he's sick, he'll need your warm, nourishing chicken soup. When he's horny, he'll desire your wildness dressed in lingerie. And when he's at a crossroads, he'll ask your wise woman for input.

Be that sweet tender maiden in the early days, to inspire his commitment. It's ok to look lovingly at a baby if you're wanting to have one. Just know when to switch gears. Feel him and feel the moment. Feel into yourself to find what's required each moment and enjoy how multi-faceted you are.

PRACTICE: Which Feminine Archetype(s) Do You Express?

Pull out a pen and write. When do you typically act as a mother, maiden, whore, crone, or something else? Which archetype(s) do you express most often? Are there ways you are currently choosing a role inappropriate to your truth and goals? Are there ways you could embody these archetypes more effectively?

Notes

Part 4

WHAT IS THE TRUE MASCULINE?

Part 4 – Introduction

Next, we'll explore masculine energy. This is again about natural qualities, and not necessarily referencing what men are programmed to be or do.

That said, Part 4 will be super helpful in understanding the guys in your life better, so you can have more successful relationships with them. On a more basic level, this will also support you in coming into your own wholeness.

By embracing your inner masculine and feminine, you'll position yourself to attract a high-caliber man who has done his inner work. If you already have a partner, this will evoke more of his greatness. Remember, it's not about neutralizing roles and being "everything all the time." Understanding these energies gives you access to the dynamic range within both you and your mate. It makes life and love more exciting and fun.

Letting go of need because you each have it all within, and yet recognizing the nuances of human expression is a recipe for elevated love. Will you say yes?

Now, let's discover the masculine…

THE RIVER AND THE RIVERBANK

One night, a couple of male friends of mine were sharing their wisdom about a subject they'd each studied for over a decade. Afterwards, one of them said, "I hope there wasn't too much 'mansplaining' tonight."

"No, I didn't have that experience," I said, surprised at his comment. While I appreciated his care and thoughtfulness, I had actually felt honored and supported that evening. I'd been very interested in what they shared.

When masculine direction comes from pure intention, as it did that night, it is a gift to the feminine. We want it! I think of our dance like a river and riverbank. While the feminine flows like a river, the masculine provides the riverbank.

The river doesn't bitch about the riverbank cramping her flow. She says, "Thank you for holding me, for being strong enough to contain all that I am." She dances against his edges and becomes more powerful in doing so.

The unhealthy masculine wills his way without consideration of our energy or feelings. This is why masculine direction gets a bad rap. Historically, many men *have* talked down to women, and women have felt misunderstood, criticized, or suppressed.

By contrast, the healthy masculine directs us only *after* first seeing us with eyes wide open. His mind is free; he does not have a pre-set, one-size-fits-all plan that he imposes on us. He directs us moment by moment, in total service, in reverence of our full creative expression.

With no riverbank, a river becomes a flood. Her chaos overtakes things. Or her water washes away in all directions and loses power.

This is where women get a bad rap for being "crazy," and why the imbalanced feminine gets nothing done. Just as our light makes his world come alive, his healthy direction supports us in effectively being all that we are.

DIRECTION

While the feminine multi-tasks, the masculine knows where he's going. Besides guiding the feminine, he climbs the ladder at work, he teaches his children, and he plays sports with clear goals.

The masculine is not nearly as complicated as we are. Forgetting this is one reason why women have such trouble in relationships! I heard one relationship coach comment that we think of them as "hairy women." Not true!

The feminine goes to a familiar restaurant and reads the whole menu. The masculine doesn't even look at the menu; he finds a good thing and sticks with it. What the feminine takes 15 minutes to say, he could say in three sentences.

Sometimes a woman feels abandoned and makes herself crazy wondering where her man is and what he's feeling, when he's simply focused on work. Things and people that fit their goals make their way into a masculine person's world. Other things don't get any attention.

His purpose is paramount. When a man feels "on purpose," he feels more powerful in every aspect of his life. Without this, it's hard for him to focus on anything else, just like we feel when love isn't flowing. In these moments, he retreats or reacts if we ask him for more love. Our best bet is to support him in knowing and achieving his purpose, giving him the space and inspiration to come around by keeping our hearts open.

DRIVE

He's more than directed. He's driven. The masculine likes and needs to achieve things, or he feels like less of a man. He likes to conquer, and that includes you.

Don't get scared. Just like the riverbank providing healthy direction to a flowing river, his "conquering" you can be a conscious, mutual dance. Overtake his ability to conquer and you may not get very far with him, if you "get him" at all.

These days, I see so many women approaching men like they're on a "hunt." Certain clients call and ask me about four men in 15 minutes. Where's the heart connection? Their pursuits often feel desperate to me.

Sometimes, a man may succumb to a woman pursuing him. But in general, they see this type of women as an "easy fuck," and then move on to someone they fall in love with, to someone who makes them feel more masculine. They want to chase us, and they don't want a woman to start directing their lives. Since the start of a relationship establishes a pattern, her initial pursuit can feel unappealing to him in the long term.

Competition with other men for your attention feels natural to him too. The masculine understands friendly competition, and so he goes out for a drink with the guy who just beat him at a race. For women, competition for love is toxic because it goes against our innate nurturing nature and reinforces the distorted feminine on the planet. So, don't compete with another woman for a man you want.

If you're a woman "looking for love," you allow him to compete and drive towards you by keeping your options open. Flirt with and even date different men, if they pursue you. I don't recommend sleeping around, but until you enter an exclusive and committed relationship, you demonstrate self-love by allowing yourself choices.

It helps you get clear on your needs and desires, and it gives the men the message that you're highly valued. This makes them want to chase; it excites their masculine. Keep your heart open and smile but don't make it too easy. This challenge is what inspires a man who's available to commit.

If you're already dating or married, he still wants to drive. It's easy to get into your comfort zone and start taking charge. While you may have aspects of your household or your life that you handle best, try not to rub his nose in it. Instead, involve him in these things as little as possible. When it comes to romance, keep some mystery so he comes looking for you.

When it comes to you, he doesn't like to lose. This is why most men choose "easier" women over amazing ones. By "easier," I don't necessarily mean easy to get in bed. I mean simpler women who don't challenge him. Men hate to disappoint us, and if he feels your standards are too high, he may go elsewhere. It can be a sign for you to relax and appreciate more, or it may mean he just doesn't share your capacity for connection.

His desire to win also applies in conversation. If you're critical, he goes into competition and the attraction gets zapped. Challenging him is good but do it from the space of knowing his capacity and inviting him there. Do it with playfulness and it turns him on.

Let him conquer you with love. Play with this dance, and your chosen man will always feel excitement when he remembers how it felt to "get you."

40 WATTS

He's simpler than you think. My psychic teachers used to compare men and women to light bulbs. If the masculine is a 40-watt bulb, the feminine is 140 watts. Neither one is better; this just explains how simple or complex we each are, and how our creative energy works.

For example, because all women are wired to make babies, we all need and have this extra "juice." Our amazing creativity is meant to go anywhere but towards a man. It's incredibly attractive when he sees it, yet incredibly overwhelming when he *receives* it. As if you plugged his 40-watt bulb into a 140-watt socket. This can cause him to lose track of his masculinity, to run away or feel crazy.

On the other hand, 40 watts feels "heavy" to the feminine. Yet it's right where he needs to be—simple, one thing at a time, bullet points. But to us it feels empty, boring, depressing. All of a sudden, we feel this way if we take on his stuff (consciously or not) in attempt to heal him. This is why I advocate regular energy clearing and balancing!

Masculine + Feminine =
Side by side make magic.
All mixed up make mud.

The dance of these energies is profound. Just listen to a choir or band. It's the low notes that make the high notes more beautiful and vice versa. This depth is almost impossible to achieve with only one or the other. And each has to be 100% itself for this to happen.

FIRMNESS

As we feel his firmness, we soften. As we relax and open, he gets hard. We crave each other and become opposites only so we can become one.

In nature, the riverbank, mountains, trees, and penetrating sun all bring firmness. Because of them, water flows, flowers grow, and people and animals light up with joy. Some landscapes are more feminine or more masculine, but all have a bit of each.

Firmness shows up in a picture frame, in a task list, or a bold statement. It's in company policies that allow more business to flow. It's in that strong massage or guiding hand. To the feminine feeling nature, it provides comfort, clarity, and support.

PRACTICE: Go into Nature and Observe the Masculine

Go into nature, put your phone away, and get quiet. If you're in a city, do your best to find a park or get out of town for a day or weekend. Notice riverbanks, rocks, the penetrating sun, the primal masculine in animals, and more. When you're done, write down what you noticed about the masculine.

Notes

PRESENCE

While the feminine radiates love and light, the masculine witnesses it. His consciousness is essential if he is to serve us. His presence is what allows him to chase a goal effectively. Too much movement or multi-tasking takes him off his game.

A feminine spiritual practice may include dancing, singing, or heart-based devotion. By contrast, the masculine sits and counts his breaths, allowing everything to fade into nothing. The part of each of us that can witness our thoughts and emotions without engaging them is the masculine part.

"This is why God invented garages," my psychic teacher used to say. The masculine needs to tinker, he needs to shut his brain off or go where it's quiet. He needs time with just men, and he needs pursuits that are all about the goal. This "sharpens his edge," so to speak.

His presence is an edge because it cuts through illusion; it penetrates our B.S. and goes straight to the heart. When we die, there will be nothing left but our heart's experience. And so, the masculine is not afraid of death, literal or symbolic. His still space of presence contains nothing and so allows everything.

When our feminine emotions inevitably erupt, a highly evolved man holds space for us. A less evolved man gets overwhelmed, runs away, or tries to "fix" or advise us. Any of these choices feel terrible to a woman, and her emotions usually intensify.

But when a man *can* offer us this space of witness—we can cry, rage, or freak out and it's done in 10 minutes. This feels so good! Like a sudden storm, we demand reverence but not reaction. A man who tries to fix our storm is a like someone trying to stop a tornado with a garden hose. If he doesn't simply drop into presence, he takes on our feelings but can't handle them.

This is why women's feelings get a bad rap. But, with awareness, it's another reminder of how masculine and feminine can truly support each other.

PRACTICE: Presence Meditation

As we get into Part 5, it will be important to embody your inner masculine at times. This way, you can best support your feminine and attract a man's consciousness.

While the feminine wakes up through embodiment, sensuality, and devotional practices, the masculine is activated through presence. So, here is a meditation to assist you in centering there:

- *Sit quietly, breathe, and ground yourself.*

- *Now, notice the part of you that is aware. No matter what's going on in your life, head, or emotions, "you" are not that stuff. As the "you" that's aware of it all, take a seat right behind your physical eyes.*

- *Imagine you're in a bubble of light or meditation room. Perhaps decorate this space as your own, so this space feels clear and light and open. It doesn't matter that your physical head is only so big. Let your sanctuary be vast enough to contain the infinite, all knowing, ever powerful, and creative being that you are.*

- *See who might be in the bubble or room with you. If there's no one, great. If you have company, ask them to honor your space and step outside. Generally, that works, but if they don't leave, ask them why they're there. Usually they want answers or something they think you have. You can let them know you'll call them later or remind them that all their best answers are in their own head, not yours.*

- *If you have a visitor that still persists, consider getting playful. Dress them in a funny outfit or play some music that drives them away, for example. It's your head so you make the rules!*

- *Notice—are there busy thoughts or conversations racing around in that head of yours? Imagine being in the "eye of the hurricane," and allow your light to simply push all of it outside your bubble for now.*
- *Stay in this space, clearing it out, or enjoying the quiet as long as you'd like.*
- *When you're done, fill in with a gold sun.*

PROTECTION

He naturally has your back. A man that doesn't do this for the women and children he loves is disconnected from his masculine side. A loving, conscious man will hold your hand crossing the street, he'll be sure your car has gas and that you go the doctor when you're sick.

On the other hand, if a man has unprocessed emotions like anger or fear or jealousy, his "protection" might come across as too intense. When my sister was in college and her two guy friends came over late at night, my dad showed up outside with an axe. He didn't know they were coming and so jumped into action when he heard them. It was his primal instinct.

Most men have bigger, stronger bodies than we do, and they have historically fought to protect and provide for us. In modern life, women don't face as many dangers, but the masculine instinct is still there. Oftentimes, it's a conscious man protecting a woman from the less conscious men out there. For example, a brother protects his sister from a toxic boyfriend. As one of my conscious male friends says, "Men need to hold other men accountable."

Meanwhile, it's best that we women don't resist his protective nature. If it's too intense or distorted, we can graciously let him know. Otherwise, our accepting his protection makes him feel good, and it brings out more of his wonderful masculine qualities.

Where Do You Receive Healthy Masculine Energy in Your Life?

Write about where you've experienced the energies mentioned in the above chapters, either from men or from life in general.

Direction

Drive

40 Watts

Firmness

Presence

Protection

Part 5

THE DANCE OF FEMININE AND MASCULINE WITHIN

Part 5 – Introduction

Now that we've explored the qualities of the true masculine and true feminine, let's consider how they work together within you. Making friends with both sides of yourself activates your creativity, brings life balance, and sets you up for success in relationships.

There's been a recent movement to awaken the Divine Feminine, which is lovely and needed, yet in the process many women have rejected their inner masculine. This has also happened in reaction to the unhealthy side of patriarchy. Unfortunately, this is impossible to sustain and just doesn't attract the best in the men around you.

On the other hand, operating from your masculine by default— because that feels safer or because the culture rewards it— tends to limit what you can receive in love and life.

Even once you embrace both sides of yourself, it can be confusing to know... When to turn on your masculine and when not to? What happens if you're in your masculine at the "wrong" moment? How do you smoothly navigate the various roles you play in life?

There's a yin in the yang and a yang in the yin. Knowing the deepest motivations of both masculine and feminine will reveal the hidden key to balance on either side. Let's discover.

EMPTINESS AND FULLNESS

The masculine in each of us seeks emptiness and the feminine in each of us craves fullness. And it's a Universal law that every empty space will be filled.

This is why we women tend to busy ourselves with conversation, food, shopping, and activity. It's the reason men turn to fishing trips, meditation cushions, or golf courses. Most men need regular time to shut the world off for a while.

If he were just like us, chattering and multi-tasking and creating constantly, we might feel safe and "at home" with him, as if we're with a girlfriend. By contrast, hearing about his solo camping trip to the wilderness on a motorcycle turns us on. We are drawn to his edge, his presence, his courage—in a very primal way. This energy in him protects us. His wildness awakens our wildness. And his consciousness penetrates our heart like nothing else.

As women, we need emptiness too. Not in the same way as men, though a little "me-time" can be really welcome. Mainly, we need a regular way to move our emotions and to release all the energy we naturally take on. When we don't do this, we tend to gain weight, get depressed, and creatively shut down.

We are meant to receive and create but we cannot do either one when we're already full. So, it takes practice and attention to keep cultivating space in our bodies and lives. Personally, I clear my energy each day through meditation, I move my body regularly, and I journal and pray as a way to feel emotions as they arise. Because emotions are stored in the body, we cannot just talk or think or visualize them away.

Just as we're drawn to a man in his emptiness, he's attracted to our fullness. Our voluptuous expression of pleasure, our creative spark, our softness pulsing open like a flower excite him.

WE ALL HAVE BOTH SIDES

Each of us has both masculine and feminine qualities. The feminine part of a man may be feeling-oriented, and the masculine part of a woman may be very driven. Ideally, each of us would embrace ALL parts of ourselves, and then *consciously* choose which qualities to express in any given moment. A woman generally needs her masculine at work, just as a father needs his feminine to nurture his children. We need a bit of each other's qualities to understand each other, and so we don't come together out of neediness.

The fun starts when you feel whole inside, because then and only then can you surrender certain parts of yourself and let your partner embody them. If they are doing the same, your energies dance together beautifully. You both feel empowered and yet elevated, so overjoyed to play together.

PRACTICE: Circulating Earth and Cosmic Energy Meditation

One great way to activate the masculine and feminine within you is to connect to both aspects in meditation. Some cultures refer to "Mother Earth" and "Father Sky," and these energies are always available. You just need to tap in. Here's a meditation to support you.

- Sit with your feet flat on the floor and spine straight. Close your eyes.
- Become aware of the spot right below your tailbone. There is an energetic center here called your root chakra, or first chakra. It allows you to feel safe in the world.
- From this root chakra, create your waterfall or tree trunk, and snuggle your hips down into your seat. Let this grounding cord be as wide as your hips and connected to both you and the center of the earth. Exhale, soften, and allow yourself to release any stress down your grounding cord.
- Rub your feet on the floor for a minute. Even with shoes on and even if you're on the tenth floor of a building, you should be able to feel a little "tingle" in the soles of your feet. There are energy centers (chakras) there as well. Think of them like spirals that begin to draw energy in from the earth, up through your legs.
- Imagine what color this earth energy is. Anything but white, brown black or grey can work-- and earth tones are often nice. Allow this colored light to flow up each leg, through the hips and the root chakra and down your grounding cord. This light is clearing and healing all the spaces it touches.
- Once you've got your earth energy flowing, it will continue as an automatic loop.
- Now, take a peek up above your head. Imagine a new stream of light flowing down through your crown. Choose any color in the

rainbow that feels inspiring and healing today.

• *Let this light continue down the back of your head and spine, cascading through two channels— left and right— all the way to the tailbone.*

• *These streams of cosmic energy converge at your root chakra, along with the earth energy that's been coming up the legs.*

• *Now, as the energies mix, imagine about 20% earth energy and 80% cosmic energy flowing up the spine, via two channels—left and right. Any excess energy at your root goes down your grounding cord.*

• *As the light coming upward reaches your heart and throat, about 10% branches out to flow down your arms and out your hands. The rest pours out the crown of your head, cleansing the space around your body before going down the grounding cord.*

• *All of this energy continues to flow on "automatic" after you activate it. I just recommend checking it once a day or when you feel "off," resetting as needed. This meditation is so healing, like an energy "shower"!*

• *When you feel ready, create a gold sun above your head. Use the gold sun as a magnet to draw your energy back from anywhere you got scattered, then let it flood your body and aura with light.*

YOUR WOUNDED MASCULINE ATTRACTS HIS

In my twenties, a guy I was dating called in excitement. "Guess what I just found in the dumpster?" he began.

Eyebrows raised, I said the obligatory, "What?"

"A new mattress!" he finished proudly.

"Ahh," I said nonchalantly. Inside, I got crystal clear. I wouldn't be sleeping over at his place.

Remembering how his hand shook as he wrote a $12 check for his share of the other night's dinner, I could imagine his thinking. He was saving hundreds of dollars perhaps, by not having to buy a mattress new.

While I wasn't in such survival myself (I had some financial assistance from my family back then), I "matched" his energy in that I had no idea how to support myself in the world at that time. I floated through my days playing music, meditating, drinking coffee, and journaling. At the time, I didn't see how my un-evolved inner masculine was attracting the same in my romantic prospects.

Around the same time, an older and wiser friend tried to set me up with a successful friend of hers. That "type" of man was so off my radar, I didn't even see what she was doing until halfway through our dinner. Needless to say, I was not interested.

Today my clients who attract "deadbeat" guys often have some healing to do in relationship to their inner masculine. Many of these women have highly evolved feminine energy, or are actively cultivating it, and can't figure out why they're attracting these types of guys.

Remember, attraction is based simultaneously in polarity and sameness. The "sameness" factor is why if you aren't dealing with your money and goals, with a healthy sense of structure in your life— he won't be either. It's practically impossible to attract something you don't have in yourself! A successful man wants your softness and radiance, yet he doesn't want you to be helpless or all over the place. He wants you to hold your own.

So, if you're one of those sensual, feminine, radiant women who can't find a successful, masculine man, have a look at your inner masculine. That may be the missing piece for you. Integrate this part of yourself and look out—magic may happen!

An upcoming Practice, "Where Do You Need to Use Your Masculine?" will help you think through this transition. But first…

LIFE SOMETIMES REQUIRES
YOUR MASCULINE

One day, I was hiking alone, and some "gangster" type of guys appeared nearby. I lived in quite a safe area, but my radar went off, and I knew it wasn't the moment to sway down the hill with a soft smile and low-cut top.

I turned on my phone and had it on hand as I ran down the trail. I kept my cool and grounded myself, yet I was driven. I knew my goal—to get out of their sight and protect myself.

Maybe these guys were harmless. However, the inner masculine in me loved me too much to take a chance.

Some women take the idea of Divine Feminine awakening too far, and they are afraid to turn on their fierceness. Listen, it's really ok. It doesn't mean you're not a radiant woman open for love. It just means you had a moment where some other energy was needed. Your empowerment is in not needing a man to provide it.

That's the moment you can choose to let him. That's the moment he can choose you, because your claws aren't sinking into him. He feels his freedom, and he feels safe to come towards you. You'll be amazed at how showing your full range as a human, while mostly being your glowing feminine self, will work wonders in his heart.

PRACTICE: Where Do You Need to Use Your Masculine?

You may need more inner masculine in handling your money, in your self-protection, life structure, or direction. Write down how you will attend to this.

Notes

WHEN HE COMPETES WITH YOU

As much as you need your healthy inner masculine to attract a great man, it's an art finding how and when to express that masculine energy. When your primary expression is masculine, he treats you like "one of the guys." He may see you as a work colleague but not as a sexual being. He may see you as a "brother" or he may compete with you.

Would you prefer to see these aspects of his masculinity—or the man in him that protects, provides, and cherishes? He has it all, just like you have many dimensions to your energy. Which parts of yourself you show him influences which parts of himself he shows you, and vice versa.

While growing up in school and in the culture as a whole, most of us got praised for our smarts and our achievements. We've learned to lead with "Here's what I do" and "here's what I think." These are mostly masculine approaches, and to a culture that has feared and repressed the feminine, they feel safer.

They have a place. But they aren't the best method for creating romance. So, if your man is competing with you, challenging you, or relating to you mentally but not emotionally or sensually—it's your job to lead the way.

It scrambles our brains, most of us... the idea that we can "lead" without thinking or doing. Trust me. Your sharing your feelings, your sensual responses, or your intuition will inspire him to change course. You lead when you do something different that inspires someone else to do something different. We women are born for this.

HOW TO SWITCH GEARS BETWEEN ROLES

A client came to me because of stress with her husband. Besides having two kids and a house to manage, they'd started a business together, and so the two were working nearly every second they were together. There were so many things that needed done, they'd stopped seeing each other as lovers!

I advised the wife to stop all work at 8 pm when the kids went to bed. At this time each night, she put on a new outfit, rubbed some essential oils on her body, and danced. Sure enough, her husband started to see her differently.

Some rare couples can pull it off, working together and maintaining romance. And many of us don't have that problem because our work or daily life is separate from our partner's. Still, it's amazing how our "work self" spills over into our personal life. Single women might easily stay in "work mode" if there's no one to go home to at the end of the day. It's especially a problem with modern technology keeping us all "on" all the time.

Most of us, men and women, use more of our masculine at work. But if you want to attract your partner's masculine energy and you're already being that—you're setting things up to either repel him, override him, or fight with him. Oops!

It may seem annoying that you have to do this but every woman I know who's followed this advice has enjoyed the end result. When you finish your workday, consciously switch gears. Jump into that proverbial phone booth, take off your business suit, and put on your Wonder Woman outfit (or whatever feminine version of yourself that you want to be that night). Bring your sensuality into this ritual, whether that means taking a shower, doing yoga, gathering flowers, or making sounds. Your man will thank you for it, and I think you'll enjoy how it makes you feel!

PRACTICE: *Act Out and Embody Your Inner Masculine and Feminine*

Have some fun with this one! No one's looking.

Go to your closet and pick out clothes that make you feel feminine. Try them on and look in the mirror, even dance a bit if you like. Experiment with different postures, tones of voice, makeup, essential oils, etc. How does the feminine you feel, look and move?

Now become your inner masculine. Which clothes, stances, thoughts or feelings best express the masculine within you?

Once you've explored each of these, you'll be ready when either energy is needed in the course of your day, because you'll remember what it feels like.

FREEDOM AND LOVE

"Come on, ravish me already!" is the psychic message so many women put out. They may not say it out loud to a man. But they tell me, and they tell their girlfriends. "Why isn't it happening?" they wail.

It goes back to your connection with love itself. If you want a man to "take you," let yourself be "taken" by life. Be in reverence of life's wonders, open to direction, soft in your heart.

By contrast, most of us close down and over-focus, especially when we're in pain. In those moments, we:

- Hold onto very specific pictures of how our relationships "should be"
- Try to "fix" the men in our lives
- Stuff our feelings, trying to maintain the illusion of control
- Resist support or guidance
- Over-analyze

In doing any of the above, we kill the thing we're trying to find. Men are attracted to women who are open, expressive, and receptive. They appreciate when we're receptive to them but it's even better when we open our hearts to life. When we do that, it's easy to be open to any one person anyway.

A woman whose life is full of wonder and adventure, who feels fully, is very attractive. A woman devoted to the God in her own heart—to love and faith in something beyond life's little details—has an easy time surrendering in love and attracting someone worthy of that surrender.

And, what the masculine most desires is not shiny hair or perky breasts or a great cook. It's freedom.

This is why lots of women try so hard on the external level and wonder why they can't keep a man. This is why when we focus more on devotion to love itself, a specific man has more space to come forward than when we focus on him or our expectations specifically.

Yes, the external is important. But when a man feels our internal freedom, on some level he feels his own and he deeply relaxes. When he is not penned in, he wants to enter!

As women, we can list all the masculine qualities that excite us, but our bottom line #1 desire is simply to feel love and life's fullness. So besides strong muscles and a good salary, if he also embraces love and life, we fall hard.

If a man is afraid of life, he'll be afraid of women, and we'll be turned off by him. By living as if he might die tomorrow, he'll realize what really matters and live his truth with courage. No woman would scare him.

Have you noticed that women love successful men? We also love men who go for their goals no matter what. It's not just about the money. Women love men who are centered in their power, fearlessly living their heart's purpose.

Because when men are strong inside, even if they don't always do what we want, we can really relax. Ahh! That's why men who bend over backwards to please women don't really please us.

As I mentioned earlier, there is a little yin in the yang and yang in the yin. Because of this, we can follow all the "rules" about being feminine or masculine and still miss something. For women, that something is having your internal freedom, even while you are feminine on the outside.

For men, the secret is internal sensitivity. With enough sensitivity, he can feel just what his woman needs and give her that in a masculine way. Otherwise, he could be the strongest man and she'd be too irritated at his cluelessness to appreciate it.

For men and women alike, the key is in the heart, in love. Letting love lead no matter what.

For the feminine, letting love lead looks more like surrender, openness, and vulnerability—with just enough discernment to choose what to open to. The Divine Masculine feels into the heart (his and others') and then acts fearlessly in service to those feelings.

If we were all the same, we might never be attracted enough to know the "zing" of love fulfilled, and that's the fun of it! On the other hand, if we forgot our hearts, we'd just be needy people drugging ourselves with externally fulfilling relationships.

Part 6

FROM "YES DEAR"
TO ANGRY FEMINISM
TO MUTUAL EMPOWERMENT

Part 6 – Introduction

Ok, we've defined the true feminine and masculine qualities. Now it's time to look at how they've been distorted or rejected. Part 6 takes us on a journey from our grandparents' ("Yes, Dear") generation through angry feminism on into today.

Here's where we look at a relationship model beyond both co-dependence and independence. What does mutual empowerment for both masculine and feminine really look like— especially if we are honoring the essence of each, and not just attempting "sameness" for the sake of equality?

Through stories, discussion, and experiential practices, this next section gives you a chance to uncover your personal relationship patterns and how they tie into larger cultural patterns. If you've been confused as to how to do things better, you're not alone!

Let me be your guide to a new way.

DISTORTIONS OF THE FEMININE

As beautiful as the true feminine can be, the distorted feminine can be ugly. Here are some of the ways it plays out:

- **Neediness.** In the "Yes Dear" era, a woman wasn't allowed to have her own work, money, or vote. No wonder women learned to be needy! Besides depending on a man for practical survival, this tendency also shows up in a woman needy for love and affection.

- **Helplessness.** Disconnected from her voice, she assumes others will read her mind instead of asking directly for what she wants. She acts like a little girl who needs rescuing.

- **Emotional manipulation.** A woman who feels disempowered shows up with a "taking" energy. At the extreme, she steals or lies to get her way. On a more subtle level, her compliments and "help" feel "sticky" or "off" somehow. Everyday conversation with her leaves you "on guard" because you sense an agenda that she's not telling you.

- **Competition and catty behavior.** Walking into a new group of women, have you ever felt "checked out" instead of welcomed? Have you experienced the pain of girls gossiping or forming cliques, or have you done this yourself? Have you felt doomed because another woman was prettier or more confident than you? It can be exhausting and devastating to always feel you'll never measure up, or to feel constant pressure to be the "best." These dynamics, along with the other distortions mentioned here, can erode your self-love and make relationships with other women feel unsafe.

- **Craziness, out of control volatility.** Women get a bad rap for being crazy, and I often think of this as the "river without a riverbank" phenomenon. Whether it's a lack of supportive men in her life, a disconnection from her internal masculine or both, feeling boundless all the time can make her crazy. On the flip side, a woman whose emotions have been repressed, perhaps due to trauma or conditioning, has a hard time expressing them in a healthy way. She either implodes or explodes.

- **Hypersensitivity.** Some women are so impressionable, receptive, and intuitive that they don't know how to manage it. It can be overwhelming to the point of us feeling crazy, over-reacting or toughening ourselves. In my younger years, I rejected and mistrusted my femininity, largely for this reason. Learning meditation and other awareness practices, like the ones I share in this book, allowed me to use my sensitivity instead of letting it use me.

- **Inappropriate mothering or caretaking.** This is where a woman is stuck in the "Mother" archetype by default, even when it's not appropriate. I remember a past partner who wouldn't let me do his laundry because he didn't want to see me as a mother figure. I appreciated his consciousness, and we never had a problem in the bedroom! By contrast, a woman who nurtures her man at every opportunity robs him of his ability to work things out for himself. She also tends to over-give, depleting herself as well as robbing herself of the pleasure and wisdom inherent in her other feminine aspects.

- **Scattered, overly superficial, or talking non-stop.** Because of the fluid, light, and changeable nature of the feminine, an ungrounded woman might seem to be "all over the place." It's like she has diarrhea of the mouth, going on and on about trivial details. She gossips and over-focuses on material things or on what others are doing. She doesn't seem to know who she is. Historically, I think this tendency stems from the lack of permission for women to live a deep life, as most got locked into the role of mother and household manager. As a result, they had to keep up with all these details.

DISTORTIONS OF THE MASCULINE

Like the feminine, masculine energy also has its dark side. I share these shadow aspects as a means of shining the light and freeing ourselves from their unconscious pull. They are sadly familiar to so many of us. Here's how the distorted masculine can show up:

- **He's overly responsible**, with the world on his shoulders. The true masculine loves to protect and provide, however sometimes he over-gives. He's the breadwinner and takes care of whatever she needs at all costs, even at the expense of his sleep, sanity, or self-care. With the exception of occasional periods of need (such as following the birth of a child), this pattern can indicate deep-seated fears around his self-worth. He may be trying to "prove it" to his dad or the culture. He may feel like he won't be loved if he doesn't "perform."

- **Avoids intimacy**. It's too scary. It might wake up feelings he's not used to feeling. He's not sure if these feelings are ok. So, he chooses "easy," shallow relationships, long-distance relationships, or none at all.

- **Insensitive and unemotional**. I get a lot of complaints about this. He has no clue what she's feeling. She pours out her heart, is obviously suffering, or has just shared for 20 minutes. He pats her on the back and changes the subject, as if to brush it all away. It's not his nature to go on and on about emotions but it IS his nature to be present. This goes for his own emotions as well as hers. If he cannot witness and hold a safe container for them, he's off-balance.

- **Domineering**. If he's uncomfortable with his inner feminine or feels unworthy as a man, he will not be able to "have" her feminine power. Faced with these feelings, a loving and conscious man will avoid her. A less evolved man will manipulate to keep her down, try to "fix" her emotions, or make them wrong, and-- at worst—abuse or control her.

- **"Grin and bear it" attitude**, where he can never be vulnerable. He goes on with what needs to be done even when he wants to collapse into a ball. He says he's "fine" when he's not. There's no one he can really talk to, really share the pain in his heart. On the same note, he guards his desire and his tenderness. He never learned it was "ok" for a man to show these types of feelings. And whether "good" or "bad," unexpressed emotions make us tense, tired, and ill.

- **Uses sex to "dump" energy into a woman**. I think this is underneath many women's complaints about sex with men. They can't put their finger on it, but they feel disconnected and used. It's not necessarily due to lack of love on his part, it's just that he doesn't know how to release his stress otherwise. The culture hasn't shown him. He might work out or yell or drink beer but that only scratches the surface. Besides sex with you, if his energy gets too bottled up, he turns to other addictions that allow him to "dump" it out.

- **Expecting a woman to cater to him**. This is same energy as in the last bullet above, only in this case you become his assistant. He dumps tasks and problems on you, expecting you to manage the house and social calendar, and also listen to his work challenges. Of course, it's lovely when partners support each other. However, it's off-balance when he expects you to do it for him at your own expense, or without reciprocation or appreciation.

- **Being a little boy needing Mommy**. Unlike my past partner who wouldn't let me do his laundry, some men are really looking for "Mommy." While this is generally subconscious, it's prevalent and shows up when he asks you for money, lacks his own direction, or is exceedingly clingy. These men are also more likely to cheat, run away, or keep their relationship options open—either because they're afraid of having no one or because they're unsure they can "man up" and be accountable in the ways we need.

DISTORTIONS OF THE RELATIONSHIP

What's the difference between healthy masculine/feminine polarity and distorted patriarchy? If the dynamic is "I do X for him and he does Y for me," that's a sign to check in. Is this pattern of relating based in choice or compromise?

Is she doing X for him because she has it in abundance to give, or because it's expected of her? Does her giving stem from her programming, his need, or her natural creative expression? Does it feel good?

It's the same for him. If "serving her" requires him to relinquish his purpose or presence or drive, he's serving her from co-dependence and not from wholeness.

If either partner expects the other to fill a hole in their lives, they are setting themselves up for disappointment. Even if it works temporarily, fulfilling someone else's need all the time is exhausting. Eventually, bitterness sets in, generally on both sides. There's no room for compromise in true love.

He can blame her for their dynamic, but it may be his pattern. She can blame him and avoid responsibility, claiming victimhood. No matter how it shakes out, there's no fault. This is epidemic and it's solved best by finding a new way.

"How can we live without compromise?" you may wonder. "Life isn't perfect."

This is where it's important to choose wisely. With a conscious partner, with a fairly developed sense of self, you have enough basis in love to find *acceptance* where things come up that you don't prefer.

True acceptance is vastly different from compromise. You retain all your life force as you accept something, and it tends to affect you less negatively.

Compromise feels bad from the very beginning. At its core, it requires division and separates you from your essential nature, not to mention from your partner and all life.

So, should you serve him a meal? That depends. Is cooking and sharing food a joy and a gift that you have? Then yes, that meal is a beautiful expression of your light. There are subtleties to this, and even a woman who loves to cook has days where she'd rather someone else do it. Those are the times to say, "I'd love to go out to dinner tonight!" Slow down and feel your feelings regularly, so you can be fluid and authentic. When you avoid getting stuck in a rut, it also gives him an opportunity to practice presence.

Even "good" partners sometimes go into default mode dictated by programming or habit, so both men and women need time to reflect. Each of you consciously embodying certain roles moment to moment is beautiful, freeing, and fulfilling when you do it. This is a practice, so please be patient with yourselves. Meanwhile, next up is an exercise to help you remember what's *not* working.

PRACTICE: How Have You Experienced the Distorted Feminine and Masculine?

Now that we've looked at some unhealthy expressions of both masculine and feminine, record some ways you've experienced each. Consider times you've personally expressed them or experienced them in your personal relationships as well as in the world around you.

Notes

HOW THE FEMININE HAS GONE UNSEEN

Over the years, this has been one of women's biggest challenges. We offer so much in terms of *energy*, which has mostly been ignored or devalued on the planet. Our love, our patience, our spiritual light, and our receptivity are all HUGE gifts to the masculine—but they are hard to measure. We can even overlook them ourselves!

Many women complain that men don't appreciate all they do. For example, your husband might take for granted the practical tasks that women have traditionally done, like cooking and cleaning. These things don't bring money in, and he's not there to see how long they take, so they may seem less important. But ask a divorced man who once had these things done for him and now doesn't! He now knows their value.

We bring that extra sparkle to everything. We give so much to our families and friends. We buy the gifts and we plan the parties. We calmly listen to his work problems, we hold the vision for his greatness, and we'll love him or push him when no one else will. But again, these "jobs" don't bring in money. They don't seem to count when someone asks, "What do you do?" at a party.

To do all we do, we need to nurture ourselves and cultivate our radiance. If you're reading this and thinking, "Radiance? What's that?" then this part is for you! We may feel guilty about taking the time and money to get massages, go to the spa, or put on makeup or a cute outfit. Yet, it's no one's fault. It's been our cultural agreement that feminine energy is less important, less seen.

At some point, most women have felt hurt by this, and we've compensated by numbing ourselves. Our pain says: why should we let ourselves feel our yearning to be cherished when we are bound to be let down?

Maybe we should pretend we don't need it? Maybe we should just "suck it up" and do all we do, whether they thank us or not?

After all, aren't we supposed to work hard to get or keep a man? Or maybe we should act like "one of the guys," like a business partner?

If only these things worked, they might be easier. But they don't!

A conscious man will recognize the value of our gifts. Meanwhile, as women, we can adore ourselves for all that we offer. As we release our self-dismissal and relax into self-worth, any man around us will start appreciating us more.

HOW THE MASCULINE HAS BEEN REJECTED

Consider all the harm the distorted masculine has done on the planet. Now think about all the anger, rage, bitterness, fear, pain, and hurt the feminine has held towards the masculine in general. Due to her emotional pain, the wounded feminine has rarely been able to see straight. It's hard for her to see the goodness in men, even when they express the healthiest of masculine energy. She takes things so seriously and blows their "mistakes" out of proportion. She shakes in fear and her fangs come out when she feels any edge at all from him.

So, he cowers. He becomes that weak, flow-y, new-age guy that worships the Goddess. He eats vegan and does yoga and speaks softly about his "process."

Imagine a good, conscious man who has healthy testosterone levels. Because he's a good man, he's aware of all the pain women have faced, and he doesn't want to cause any more of it. His masculine may feel pushed away and rejected by the wounded feminine.

He may wonder, "Is it ok to tell her she looks nice?" "Can I ask her out or should I 'respect' her space?" He may feel some raw, primal desires that he's pretty sure she wouldn't be "ok" with. And so, he turns to porn, masturbation, or an "easy" woman whom he has little connection with.

Does this nurture anyone's heart? Of course not. Does this give women what they really want? No, it's simply a Band-aid. It increases separation between men and women. And it hurts because it dishonors and suppresses life force.

As for this "good" man… if he's lucky, he has a few close friends to talk with. Even better, he has a men's group or a mentor. But if he's like many men, he doesn't have anyone he can be "real" around, just guys he can chat with about work and sports or have a drink with. Our culture hasn't offered much in the way of healthy masculine role models. When it comes to the tough stuff, men are supposed to "man up." Vulnerability is seen as a weakness.

I am seeing a new wave of men's groups and programs teaching skills for the healthy masculine. It seems that we have a long way to go before most men have this type of support. Meanwhile, understand that your guy may be hurting inside, just as you've been. Your compassion means more to him than you know.

PRACTICE: How Have You Experienced the Rejected Masculine?

Have you ever rejected the masculine? Have you seen this happening in your environment? Or, have you noticed this in the men around you? Reflect on your experiences here.

Notes

MEN'S SENSITIVITY IS KEY

I'd been talking to some male friends about this book, and about how the Divine Feminine *wants* the Divine Masculine to come forward. In the same conversation, we were talking about different ways of relating and I mentioned I was "tactile." I was simply telling stories, as we all were.

At the end of that night, one man who was new to our community reached out and touched my shoulder on our way out. That alone would have been ok, but it continued for the next week. Every time he got within reach of me, even when I didn't say hi or look at him or anything, he touched me. I had zero romantic interest in him, and I thought that was pretty clear. It got to the point where I started positioning myself on the other side of the room so it wouldn't happen.

After a few days of my dodging him, I ended up standing where he could get to me. I was in a deep conversation with someone else, and he walked up and touched me again.

"No, thank you," I said as I backed away.

He looked shocked. I could hardly believe he was so clueless. I realized I had to talk with him about it.

As we walked out, I said I needed to be direct about something. After appreciating his seemingly good intentions, I told him the repeated touch made me uncomfortable. I explained that I wasn't energetically participating and so I felt he was coming at me. He apologized and I told him I sensed it was simply his unawareness, which he acknowledged.

This particular man had a "stunted" energy when it came to relationships. There was a stiffness in his body, perhaps due to his own trauma or from trying too hard to be a "man." I don't know because I don't really know him. However, this experience was enlightening for me and it brought me a new awareness.

It showed me that masculine sensitivity is key. It is what determines whether the bold masculine sweeps a woman off her feet or assaults her with inappropriate gestures. It is what keeps the masculine pure and enlivening, not distorted and threatening.

It's important that we support our men in being sensitive. This doesn't mean coddle them or ask them how they feel all the time. Instead, be absolutely sure to give them space and support when they show emotions. This also means to respond immediately and generously when they do or don't display sensitivity *to us*.

A man who feels his woman moment to moment is an amazing lover. In or out of bed, let him know when he's on track—for example, when he gets you the most thoughtful gift or gives you a break from the kids when you need it most.

By contrast, if your guy takes you to a party on the night you're exhausted, or if he insists on doing another hour of errands before dinner when you're starving, go ahead and show your displeasure. One way that men develop sensitivity is through our feeling responses. If you're with an insensitive man, tune in and ask yourself if he truly doesn't care or just needs to learn.

Many men have no idea we want them to be sensitive, or that the benefit is that they get to be uber-masculine once they are. Sensitive is sexy. You can let him know.

THE COLLECTIVE MYTH THAT MEN
ARE DISAPPOINTING

I remember about the thirtieth time I heard myself telling the story. It was in my friend Leeta's shop. I walked into the scent of her essential oils, carrying my then-infant daughter asleep in her pouch, and I found Leeta there with a client, another woman I knew.

"How's it going?" one of them asked me.

"It's stressful. Arthur's not making enough money. He's just sitting on the couch chanting and looking at his iPad, and I'm the one working and cooking and and…" I stopped.

The client was just looking at me, not agreeing, just holding very neutral. But I saw what I was doing.

I didn't say anything at the time, I just dropped my story. And in that moment, I decided not to repeat the story anymore.

These women were intuitive too. They could feel it, I'm sure. I was energizing the situation I said I didn't want through my beliefs and words. There was some part of me attached to doing it.

When I examined this, I realized there's been a long-standing agreement amongst women that says men are disappointing. It's been true for many of us. We bond over it.

Even though it's starting to change, many of us have deep-seated fears of losing the love from our mothers, our ancestors, or other women if we break this pattern. We're afraid to break ties or be disloyal. We're afraid of upsetting our friends by choosing not to agree to their stories.

Occasionally, I get a client like this. She wants me to agree to her story because it somehow comforts her. It's part of my job to say, "I hear that story… I've been there… Do you want to keep telling it or do you want a change?"

In my case, I stopped telling the story and as the years went on, Arthur became more and more successful and supportive—financially and in every way. He had always wanted to. My disengaging from the programs that said otherwise helped him do this in the time we were together.

MOVING BEYOND TRANSACTIONAL
RELATIONSHIPS

I get why women are disappointed, even outraged. In my grandmother's generation, a woman gave up so much of her own identity to be with a man. Most of them couldn't work outside the home if they wanted to do so. Almost all their creativity went into their families. Their money came from men, so they had little power to leave a bad situation. If they were lucky, he was kind and provided well. Few had the support to fully express themselves. The unlucky ones suffered incredibly. Probably the worst of it was that women hardly knew what they were missing. How can you imagine what you've never had, and don't see anywhere around you?

In those days, relationships were mainly transactional. She raised the children and he went to work. She gave him sex and he gave her money. She gave him support and he gave her status.

I still hear remnants of this mindset today, even in conscious people. For example, one of my clients yearned for her man to understand her better. She told me her plan to change it, which went something like this: "Please give me A and I'll give you B." While that sounded so reasonable, I knew he would resist her giving him "directions." Besides, it didn't speak to his heart.

Instead, I suggested she give him a feeling-message about her experience. For example, "I know you love me. But when you look at your phone while I'm talking to you, I feel like I'm just talking to myself. I can do that all day long. I had so much fun with you that day we went out and you forgot your phone!"

That way, she's not telling him what to do, she's simply *responding* to his different behaviors. It's almost a suggestion but the difference is that she's *giving* by sharing feelings instead of *taking* charge with her mind. Once he replies, she can then *ask* him what he needs from her, instead of prematurely assuming she knows.

That common phrase "It's a give and take" is old paradigm! I prefer "give and give." This way, each person is empowered and valued as they share. And both get to receive—not from need, but just because it feels good.

PRACTICE: *Clearing Energy Cords*

Every relationship comes with spoken and unspoken expectations. In the example above, my client was thinking of directly asking for different behavior (I'll give you this and you give me that). Our unspoken agreements can be just as—if not more—problematic.

Energetically, I see these agreements as "cords" between two people. We might have cords in the heart, in the tailbone (survival) area, in the low belly (sexual) center, or other places. Depending on where the cord is, you'll know the nature of the agreement.

Generally speaking, ongoing cords between adults are not helpful, and they can definitely cause problems. We may lightly create a cord in moments of close connection but then it ideally gets released. Often, cords are subconscious and invisible until we meditate on them or ask a healer to assist us. Cords indicate binding. They are a clear indicator that some part of you has agreed to a transactional, need-based relationship.

NOTE: Energy cords are necessary between a parent and dependent child. These cords should not be removed, and they may even need strengthening from time to time.

Here's a meditation to discover and release any cords between you and others:

- *Sit in a comfortable, meditation space and close your eyes.*
- *Create your grounding cord, exhale, and feel yourself "land" in your body.*
- *In your minds' eye, scan yourself for any cords. Check both the front and back of your body. You might easily see the cords. Alternately, be aware of any feeling of a cord plugging into you. This sometimes feels like a "pinch," an energy "leak," or a dull pressure. It's possible you have no cords but most of us have some.*
- *Once you get a sense of a cord connected to you, ask yourself who's*

on the other side. You might see someone's image pop into your mind, you might trace the cord to the other end, or you might just feel or know who it is. Whether or not you know who it's from, you might have a sense of what it's about. See whatever you notice.

• Do NOT remove any cord between you and a dependent child. If it's between you and another adult, ask yourself if you're ready to release this cord. If not, be kind to yourself and check back later. Otherwise, you can take your hand to the cord and "imagine" gently twisting it out. What happens on the other end is up to the other person, so don't worry about their part. Once you've got it out of you, there are a couple more steps to take.

• Imagine a gold sticky rose and run in through the spot where the cord was. Let the rose absorb any energy in you that says you need that cord. Notice what colors, pictures, or messages pop into your head as you do this. When you feel complete, send the rose off to the edge of the horizon and see it go "poof" in your mind's eye.

• Finally, fill the space where the cord was with gold light, or any other color that represents your wholeness and balance. This last step is important, so you don't repeat the pattern.

• Enjoy, and feel free to do this with any additional cords!

DE-TANGLING FROM MIXED SURVIVAL MESSAGES GIVEN TO WOMEN

On the one hand, we women have been taught "You need a man to survive." That was certainly the case in our grandparents' generation, and still is true for many. But since feminism made it popular to fight for our independence, and since many women have come out with stories of abuse or harassment, we have a new survival message to contend with. It says: "You won't survive if you need a man."

What's a woman to do? Our feminine self might like to receive from a man. It might feel good if he pays the bills or protects us from potential danger.

Our independent self might reject our feminine desire to receive. She says, "What if I rely on him for money and then he cheats or hits me or puts me down? Then I'm screwed. What if I lose myself? It just feels safer to be in control of it all."

Whether you're in a "Yes Dear" relationship or an angry feminist, this issue is the same. It's about finding security within first and foremost. When you're rooted in self-love, these survival fears no longer apply. As you connect into your feelings, you will *know* when you're with a man capable of honoring you in all ways. As you explore the exercises in this book, you'll un-hook from unhealthy transactional relationships. You may need to do something or shift something in your energy or way of relating but that will be *because* you've already chosen to find a new way. I trust this is why you're here.

MOVING BEYOND ANGRY FEMINISM

In the 90s, I went to UC Santa Cruz, a progressive hippie mecca. There, I cannot count how many times I heard something like "Dismantle the hetero-patriarchal phallocentric" blah blah blah. It was very uncool to be a feminine woman or a masculine man.

Between this, my mom's complaints about my dad, and my own pain with boyfriends, it became easy to blame the masculine. Eventually, I became a singer/songwriter with heroes like Ani DiFranco and Alanis Morissette, and I joined an organization called indiegrrl (note the growl in "grrl"!).

Now, I am all for strong women and I love those artists but there was definitely an imbalance for me at that time. Rather than expressing the strength that came from my wholeness, I suppressed my own feminine and rejected the masculine around me. I became a "warrior," thinking that meant a man couldn't hurt me. Never mind how I hurt myself by putting up so many walls.

I understand, following the age of "Yes Dear," how important it was for women to go to work, to vote, and to claim all the rights that men had. But, as I see it, the pendulum swung too far.

If you're currently angry with men, if you're anxious or even terrified, you may need to feel these things fully before moving on. In the case of past trauma—large or small—you probably went "numb" when it happened and so your feelings got pushed down. Feeling blah, holding extra weight or resentments, being edgy or protective are signs you're holding stuff you didn't feel safe to process in the first place.

A common fear is that dredging up long-lost pain will cause the trauma to happen again. The truth is the opposite. Once you finally and safely feel it, you'll be free of it for good. So, explore your emotions, and express them in a healthy way. You don't have to understand what they're about to heal them; in fact, you probably don't want to remember all the details. That would be like following the trash truck down the street to see what you threw out.

How do you access feelings that got stuck? You can journal, dance, cry, receive bodywork, or beat a pillow. Because of the power of your emotions, set your intention to express them for the purpose of healing, with harm to none. Light a candle, say a prayer, or do a visualization along these lines—whatever makes sense for you.

Then, let it rip. Don't censor anything from here. If you need to scream, scream from your heart and stay open. Let yourself tremble or wail. Dive into the middle of the pain with your whole body. Be willing to get to the edge of it. Be open to the message or feeling on the other side.

Starting from movement or meditation can help. If your mind is stuck in a toxic loop, going to the mirror and saying those thoughts "to your face" can bring their ridiculousness to light. Exaggerating things like you're an actress can shake the stuck-ness out of you. Beyond all of this, sometimes we need a friend or trained professional to help us see and heal the hard stuff.

I see a new wave of anger at men in the #MeToo movement. And it's healthy for the shadow to come to light. Women who've been victimized need to voice it and heal. Men who haven't been accountable need to come clean. Both the distorted feminine and masculine energies have contributed to this problem. We've all been confused and ultimately a healthier way is ahead.

You cannot get beyond something until you feel it fully. To attempt this is spiritual bypassing. So, go ahead, pause, and give yourself some TLC if emotions are coming up around all this.

IMPORTANT TIP: If you feel like you can't shake certain emotions no matter what you do, you may be feeling things that aren't yours. Cry your own tears and you feel better. Express your own anger and you get clear. Take on someone else's feelings and it's like trying to put the wrong puzzle piece in your puzzle. It will never fit, you'll try forever, and the other person will also be stuck. You can never process what's not yours. We sometimes take on emotions from family, friends, or the culture, so check this in yourself. The next exercise will help.

PRACTICE: How to Feel Your Emotions and Release Those that Aren't Yours

Consider a relationship challenge or some difficult emotions you're experiencing.

- *Sit or stand, breathe and ground.*
- *Imagine a gauge that shows you 0 to 100%. This might look like the gas gauge in your car, and it might be old-fashioned or digital.*
- *Looking at the gauge, ask, "How much of what I'm feeling here is mine?" Note the answer from 0 to 100%.*
- *Take note of your answer.*
- *Assuming you got less than 100%, imagine a bubble a few feet in front of you—like a magic soap bubble with a magnet in it.*
- *Allow the bubble to pull all that energy out of you that's not yours. You don't have to figure out what it is or where it came from, though you might get a sense.*
- *Just focus on the energy releasing, and your intention will make it happen. Exhale and notice if the bubble changes color or anything in this process.*
- *When you feel complete, see the bubble float off to the edge of the horizon and dissolve into a burst of light.*
- *As this happens, the energy you were holding goes back to whomever or wherever it came from, creating a healing for all concerned.*
- *Fill in with a gold sun and come out of meditation.*
- *Assuming you got more than 0% on your gauge, and that some of the emotions ARE yours, let yourself feel them. Cry, yell, shake, write, tell someone, punch a punching bag... find an appropriate way to release the feelings and you'll feel better on the other side.*

"YES, MY LORD."
HOW TO HANDLE HIS PATRIARCHAL WAYS

It's a fine line between him being a strong, protective, inspiring man and him being too domineering. Men sometimes get confused about how to be, and they have generally learned more patriarchal behavior from their ancestors and from society. Occasionally they *are* jerks on purpose but often they override us just because that's familiar behavior.

How do you handle something like this? How do you teach him to act differently, without taking on a competing masculine or mothering role?

One way is through play. If your man gets too bossy, you can say, "Is there anything else you'd like, My Lord?" This calls him out on his behavior without taking a "direct" approach or coaching him. It keeps you in the feminine role, and it invites his masculine to enjoy a challenge. It brings awareness to how he's being but without confronting or criticizing him. If he's a fairly conscious man, he'll laugh and change his tune.

TRUE FREEDOM AS A WOMAN

Just as sensitivity is key for men, internal freedom is an empowered woman's secret. Contrary to the pseudo "freedom" espoused by angry feminism, true freedom for a woman means she is rooted in wholeness. Her connection with something larger than herself along with her natural feminine and masculine means her life force flows freely. Because she represses nothing, others' imbalances have no pull to sway her. Her self-love provides all the protection she needs.

Even more so, her inner freedom draws in the healthy masculine. Remember that the masculine desires freedom more than just about anything. If a woman pushes to feel hers, she comes from a "fighting" space and so inspires his competition. However, if a woman is genuinely free inside, it brings any man around her a huge sigh of relief. He gets something he deeply needs simply by feeling her "vibe." It's not conscious but it's palpable and very powerful.

GIVE AND GIVE

We are coming full circle. After recognizing that yes, women are equal to men, we can relax into remembering our differences.

Some of the gifts we give our partners are Universal masculine and feminine qualities, such as direction and flow or firmness and softness. Other gifts are based in our individual personalities, regardless of gender. For example, one partner likes to cook and the other likes to clean. One's steadfast and organized and the other connects them to new friends and adventure.

On the surface, our new paradigm relationships may appear just as transactional as our grandparents' "Yes Dear" relationships. The difference is subtle yet profound. The difference is in knowing our wholeness yet *choosing* to embody certain qualities and relinquish others. We are not needy anymore, and so we give and receive from our joy.

Even though I have an inner masculine drive and direction, it doesn't excite me to drive when going on a date. I like to ride and let my man drive! And while I appreciate his sensitivity, I don't want to always have to hold it together while he cries or yells on a regular basis.

I like to cook, and in one relationship, I felt disappointed when my boyfriend wanted to cook with me. I wanted to give that gift! It was amusing and illuminating to see this in myself.

PRACTICE: What Would You Like to Give and Receive in a Romantic Relationship?

Write down the gifts you have to offer your current or envisioned partner? What would you love to share? What would you love to receive from him?

Notes

Part 7

OVERCOMING THE COLLECTIVE
FEAR OF FEMININE POWER

Part 7 – Introduction

Fear of feminine power is a wound we all carry to some degree. It's epidemic, and it's been at the root of both feminine repression and distortion. It's also why "equality" has seemed so tempting.

This is not the same as fear of women. We can be scared of the feminine in men just as easily. And simply putting women in positions of power does not address the issue if they are not modeling feminine energy.

In practice, fear of the feminine shows up as female competition, repressing our feelings or beauty, inability to relax or receive, overly taming our less "agreeable" sides, and creating shadows around sexuality.

If you're ready to bust through these patterns and be one of the brave pioneers to wave the light beam for others, let's go. I'm by your side.

MOST PEOPLE ARE AFRAID OF FEMININE POWER

One reason so many women try to feel powerful by acting like men is because feminine power is THAT powerful. It's scarier than masculine power, in a way. Volcanoes, hurricanes, and earthquakes are expressions of this power. No man or woman wants to mess with that.

Our culture has manipulated the feminine in unfortunate ways. On the one hand, we see sex symbols everywhere, and there is the billion-dollar porn industry. Then in daily life, women hide their feelings, hold back their radiance, and act like men.

No wonder men are jacking off in front of iPads and avoiding their wives! Ladies, is this what you want? It's becoming easier, in a sense, for men to avoid a "real" relationship. This is one of the reasons you are needed, to inspire something more in him.

You might say, "That's not my job." And you're right, in some cases. Some men aren't up for raw and real intimacy. But a good, conscious man yearns to feel your heart. On his own, he lacks your light, and he cherishes it fully when you offer it.

Even the most evolved man will have his moments. He'll want to disappear and not be faced with all that you are. He'll want to shrink from the challenge. And your shining heart, beckoning him back to his edge, is sexier than any porn star in this moment.

HOW MISTRUSTING THE FEMININE
HAS HURT US

So many feelings come up in the process of awakening our feminine! For instance:

"If I show my feminine radiance, will it trigger my mom? Will it make her feel bad about her looks? Will she judge or control me? What if my dad pays more attention to me than to her?"

"Will my sisters, friends, or other women be jealous? I want a guy, but I want the women in my life to love me too. Help!"

"Should I wear the dress I look really hot in or not? Am I manipulating a man if I do this / wear this / say this? Am I making him uncomfortable?"

"I don't want to be less respected. I should probably just show him how smart I am, dress conservatively, and talk about 'safe' subjects like work."

All of these common thoughts are evidence of how wounded our feminine has been. As women, we're damned if we do and damned if we don't. And the byproduct is a forced, awkward, overly mental approach to how we carry ourselves.

No matter whether you wear that dress or not, whether you let your sensuality flow or not, if you are *also* worrying about it, you'll create a less desirable response. These worries are already in the collective. You don't need to repeat them, so see what happens if you just drop them and ask yourself, "What feels most natural and appropriate in this instance?"

To a large extent, your worries are what make other people feel uncomfortable. They feel the gap between how your body looks and what your energy is saying. If your body and outfit is saying, "Fuck me," but your energy says, "I feel really awkward and I hope this is ok what I'm wearing," you're not that fuckable. In fact, you've just opened yourself to the same judgement you're directing towards yourself.

Once I went to a workshop on sexuality and spirituality, and we were asked to wear something on Day 3 that made us feel feminine. I brought a red dress that I planned to wear on that day. By the time Day 3 came, I wore it and felt completely awkward. I had shifted so much energy through the workshop that *that* dress felt like a forced expression of femininity. It didn't align with my deeper feminine heart.

We all know the Adam and Eve story. There is the whole idea that a woman can "ruin" a man. This is because feminine energy *can* be very distracting when a man is in his masculine. This is why it really benefits men to cultivate their capacity to witness and control their energy.

We all have the Adam and Eve story somewhere in our consciousness, and most of us women have either internalized it and repressed ourselves or rebelled by being overly sexual. In spite of our intentions, the latter can feel disconnected and repelling. Most of us have done both.

There is a third way. When we don't worry about how we come across as women, and just do what's natural, we can wear sweats and still shine with radiance. And when we "turn it up," we feel juicy inside; we're not just dressing up or flirting because we "should" or because we need to cover up our anxiety. Then our sexiness is attractive and feels natural in its powerful expression.

Your capacity to feel a lover in bed is the same sensuality that allows you to feel yourself and your environment. It knows what's appropriate in any given moment. So, practice feeling everything whenever you feel safe to do so, and it will definitely pay off with your man!

PRACTICE: Sound, Dance, Move

One of the best ways to awaken your feminine power is to move your body! Find a time when no one's around, or practice with a girlfriend or women's group. Put on something comfortable and turn on your favorite music. Let your body move any way it wants to move. Do this as a prayer, as a way to move stuck energy and open up your creativity.

BEAUTY IS NOT SUPERFICIAL

Years ago, I moved to LA and joined a high-end yoga studio with famous teachers and students. There I learned to merge beauty and spirituality.

Previously, as a singer-songwriter in Boulder, Colorado, I remember preparing for a photo shoot for my CD cover art. The photographer suggested I wear my own makeup to the shoot. "I don't have any makeup," I said proudly. It was true! I had adopted these hippie values that said everything "natural" was better.

Actually, indigenous people have been painting their face with "natural" materials for millennia. It's innate in the feminine to adorn herself and want to look pretty. I did it as a young girl, looking at fashion magazines and curling my hair. Why was it that the "feminism" I adopted in my twenties didn't allow makeup?

Those women in LA's yoga studios showed no shame in dressing in sexy, beautiful outfits, wearing makeup and doing their hair. As an artist and spiritual seeker, their flair and style appealed to me. It showed me the power of including "the world" in my spirituality. For truly, spirituality is about union.

My previous idea of that union assumed that masculine and feminine don't matter. In nature and in human life though, it's a real thing. At this point, I prefer to unite by embracing the masculine and the feminine, not by avoiding it. Beauty is a Divine quality. Makeup is just one example.

STOP COMPETING

You may have jealous feelings about other women. This can look like behaviors such as fearing your partner or love interest is interested in his attractive friend or co-worker, wanting to look better than your friends when going out, or comparing your body with other women's bodies at the beach or pool.

These are common and useful to notice because they have a message for you. By indulging them, you feed the collective mistrust of the feminine and it's bound to come back at YOU. Your ego may think otherwise but you cannot simultaneously have negative thoughts about other women and also love your own femininity.

My friend, Marla Mervis-Hartmann, who coaches women around body image and self-love, says we should appreciate both ourselves and the women around us. I'll never forget one day we hung out at her house. I got up to get something and she said, "Ann, you have a nice butt." How often do straight women say these things to each other? But she was very pure and sincere.

If you have trouble appreciating other women or if you have frequent jealous feelings, your self-worth may need a boost. Every emotion has a message, and whatever we're jealous of in another usually shows us something we've disowned in ourselves. On the other hand, judging another woman usually means you're projecting your self-judgement onto her. So next time you feel jealous or judgmental, use your feelings as a tool to adjust your relationship with yourself!

PRACTICE: *Appreciating Yourself and Other Women*

On the following pages, list ten things you appreciate about yourself, then ten things you appreciate about other women.

Ideally, this writing practice will move you in the direction of appreciating other women in daily life. You don't have to complement your friends' butts out loud if that's not in your comfort zone, but at least note to yourself when you see a beautiful woman on the street. Feel her radiance, and as you do, allow your own radiance to expand. More than likely, she'll start to shine even more because everyone is psychic. And you will definitely light up!

Things I appreciate about myself:

1.

2.

3.

4.

5.

6.

7.

8.

9.

10.

Things I appreciate about other women:

1.

2.

3.

4.

5.

6.

7.

8.

9.

10.

HOW TO SHOW FEMININE POWER WITHOUT BEING BLATANTLY SEXUAL

If you've been hiding your body, sensuality, or light your whole life, you might feel like flaunting it. On the other hand, if sexual attention triggers discomfort, you might inadvertently limit your experience by holding back parts of yourself. If you're wanting a man's attention, is it appropriate to dress sexy and flirt, or not? Much of this depends on what feels good and authentic to you, and each man has his preferences as well.

I have heard some say that a woman in clothes is sexier than a naked body—perhaps because of the fun imagining what's underneath the clothes. Showing too much can look like you're giving it away or are insecure and overcompensating—giving you a "lower value" in his eye. And because the masculine likes to "conquer," a woman who "lets it all hang out"—or who tries too hard—can be a turn off.

On the other hand, years ago I was told by a boyfriend that I did a "good job of hiding" my body. It's common for image consultants to recommend dressing in clothes that flatter one's figure. It's possible to do this in a classy way. Cover it up too much and you shortchange the world from experiencing your beauty!

Both hiding your body and being overtly sexual can be signs of deep wounds around your femininity. Hiding it all the time says, "I don't feel safe," "I'm scared," or "I'm angry, so fuck it—you can't have any of this and I don't need it either."

Dressing, talking, and oozing sex can say, "I'm desperate for attention." It might indicate "I don't feel good about myself. This is all I got, so I better 'put it out' in order to get somewhere in life." I have also observed women provoking attention by dressing sexy, and then blaming the men. "How dare you check me out? How dare you make those comments?"

I myself was guilty of this. After hiding my body for years, the pendulum swung the other way and I felt a need to wear low-cut tops and perform sexually suggestive songs and poems. Did that make it ok when a man sat there touching himself in a low-lit bar where I was singing? No. But I had to look at what I had to do with it. I had started "owning" my sexuality but still had issues that played out in these uncomfortable experiences.

I remember seeing a friend of mine naked in a sauna. She had done tons of meditation, energy clearing, and spiritual work on herself—including on her sexuality and feminine energy. And when I saw her body, it literally glowed. It felt clear, pure, and innocent—her own. Ever since that day, I have regularly cleared the energy around my sexual space in meditation, and I've assisted other women in doing so. Often, we hold past sexual traumas in our physical bodies. These can include rape or abuse, lustful stares and other people's fantasies, repeated sex with a partner you resent, or the pain of longing for a lover who left. Until the energy is cleared, it profoundly affects your sexuality and body.

What we wear or say is only part of the equation. The energy we broadcast comes back to us, like it or not. Sometimes we aren't conscious about what we're putting out, so this is an art to develop.

What you're thinking also matters. I was once listening to a talk by David Deida, and he answered a woman's question about how to indicate in public that you're single and looking—without attracting the wrong kind of attention. His answer was to repeat in your mind, "I would give myself totally to the *right* man." The important key here was inviting the "right" man, not just "any" man.

Back then, I was single, and tried this at the grocery store and other public places. It certainly gave me a fun feeling of anticipation—I was open and confident, and it definitely seemed like I attracted better potential partners.

Using your feminine power of attraction is an art. Some art is subtle, and some is dramatic. It's up to you to feel into what's needed in any given moment. This moment, what feels like an accurate expression of your heart? For each occasion, for each person, what kind of gift from you feels appropriate to give? Find the gift that comes from a natural, non-needy place within you. Sense what gift would be welcome and well-received. For truly, you are that gift.

ARE YOU "HOOKING" HIM?

In the new paradigm of give-give relationships, any kind of manipulation only backfires. This includes dressing overly sexy to feel powerful or worthy, playing games to get "love" or attention, or turning him on as a passive-aggressive move. While these tactics can work in the short term or with a less conscious man, they ultimately push away any man you'd really want.

In your attempts to attract his love, are you drawing him in or "hooking" him? He's not a fish and the last thing he wants is to feel trapped. Remember, the masculine qualities include "drive" and "direction." It's difficult for him to do that if you're doing it for him.

You may wonder how to distinguish leading from your feminine with driving him into a corner. It's about keeping it clean, leading from having rather than from needing. Your natural feminine leadership allows for honest, open-hearted communication. It's actually your responsibility as a woman to offer this. It allows him to feel safe doing the same.

WHEN YOU FEEL AFRAID OF MEN, KNOW THIS

My spiritual teacher of ten years once said in a seminar, "Ladies, when you feel afraid of a man, he's probably afraid of you." Because he was a psychic and a man, in a room full of mostly women, his words packed a punch. I was grateful for his honesty and I felt the truth in his words.

Though men act strong on the surface, society generally requires them to appear this way. History has enforced the story that women are vulnerable and so should fear men. But after doing intuitive readings for thousands of women, I have seen how often their male partners or love interests get scared.

All the time, I hear questions like "Why did he pull away?" "Why did he break up with me?" "Why does he say those hurtful things?"

I've given so many of these women a similar answer: "He's scared. He feels intimidated by you. He's afraid he can't measure up. He'd rather leave you before he's left. He feels useless when you're unhappy. He'd rather dominate you before you overpower him."

When I'm out walking alone and see men, sometimes I do feel vulnerable. In those moments, I remember this truth. All kinds of men get scared of our power, our light, of their own repressed desire and dark sides.

I don't need to be afraid if I can see this and stay soft and centered around it. My anxiety, defensiveness, or fear might only make it worse. So, I stay in a space of neutral acceptance and say to myself, "I bring out the best in all men." As I do so, frequently these men show a sudden kindness, respect, and relaxation I hadn't seen moments before.

Everyone is psychic, and our power to project is just as great as our power to receive. It's exciting to me that we can use it for such good.

SUPPRESSING SEXUAL ENERGY CAUSES PROBLEMS

My client had just ended a long-term relationship after having an affair. He was struggling with what to do about the new woman, who was already talking about marrying him. Feeling smothered, he expressed his desire to pull away from her.

I saw that this woman gave him an energy that he needed. I was talking with him from my New Mexico home after a month of 95-degree days with no rain, so I described it like "Imagine living in the desert then getting a vacation to the coast of Northern California. If you lived there all the time, it wouldn't be as special." Her energy was like medicine to him; it gave him something he'd been missing.

It looked like his new relationship wouldn't serve him long-term, and I saw his desire to "man up" and walk away. Yet he wasn't able to. Why?

Until he recognized the medicine she provided, he was bound to her. Until he admitted and allowed himself to fully feel his desire and appreciation for her, it controlled him. When he pushed her away, he inevitably pushed away even the stuff he liked, and some wise part of him didn't want to do that.

I gave him two homework assignments: (1) Write her a letter expressing his feelings for her, then rip it up; (2) Own what he loves about her, and then put those qualities on his "wish list" for his next partner.

Every woman has different qualities and energy. It's rare that one woman is going to have everything a man wants (or vice versa). Until we own our true sexual feelings and desires, we tend to either act them out inappropriately (in this man's case, by having an affair), or by repressing everything—including our potential for fulfillment and pleasure.

Within a conscious partnership, we can admit or even share these feelings, and redirect them into the relationship. Without a lover, we can explore letting ourselves feel everything without judgement. Our acceptance brings light to our "shadow" side, and then it's much easier to choose appropriate action. In every case, there are ways to get the energy one desires while honoring everyone involved.

It's amazing how when we stop censoring ourselves, we naturally self-regulate. Our true natures are good, and our sexuality is part of this!

I have also seen women get sick when their sexual energy is repressed. At the very least, they become anxious and tight in their bodies. Some get dry, hormones get wonky, and sex becomes painful. An extreme manifestation might be cancer, reproductive disorders, or serious illness.

POLITICALLY CORRECT GENDER NEUTRALIZATION

Not long after moving to New Mexico, I found myself giving women makeovers in my mind. I missed how the women shine in LA, and not just the rich and famous! There, women of all types at least seemed to *care* about their appearance. I'm sure I was seeing this because of what I was working through, awakening to the Divine Feminine aspects of beauty.

When my dad came to visit Santa Fe, I asked him, "What do you think of the women here?"

He replied immediately, "Old and worn out."

Then I had lunch with a male friend, who said he was struggling to meet women there. He said, "The women here look like they don't want to get laid. At least they could wear clothes that fit."

When I first arrived in Santa Fe, it seemed the men had never seen a woman before. I realized quickly that if I went out wearing tight jeans and makeup (required attire in LA), heads would turn. One day, I was home wearing a skirt with sequins on it and my male neighbor came by.

"Is that what you wear around the house?" he exclaimed.

I said, "Yes, I wear what I feel good in."

At the time, the men there felt very airy, very loose in their boundaries. Yes, lots of them were "spiritual" but I couldn't feel their firmness as men. The women felt hardened, and the men softened, and sometimes I couldn't tell them apart. I got the feeling they thought they were progressive, but they actually seemed reactive. I don't think they meant to be.

Our history of patriarchal oppression made these reactions understandable. Many women feared that their feminine energy would make them unsafe. Men who didn't want to harm women chose to go passive. Thankfully, there are other options!

Politically-correct gender neutralization is just as harmful—and, in fact, accomplishes the same thing—as overt patriarchy. Living as if our light is not there and doesn't matter hurts us. Many times, we don't even know why we're suffering, because of the assumed compromise in our culture. In the face of pain without understanding, we go numb.

When men repress their desire for our light, that's when their energy comes out in distorted ways. Some have affairs, some become passive-aggressive (or just plain aggressive), some turn to addictions or fantasy. They go numb just like we do because they're not ok with themselves or us. This is no way to live, and obviously a world of numb people affects more than just our relationships and sex lives.

MEN'S VIOLENCE REFLECTS WOMEN'S REPRESSED WILDNESS

I believe that we all—deep-down—seek love and healing for ourselves and others. Whether we consciously choose this or not, our instinctive selves keep doing what needs to be done to create balance. We act out the shadows, trying to bring them to light.

I don't condone men's violence; it can be incredibly damaging. And yet, on a collective level, I see it as a warped attempt to somehow express an energy that needs to be expressed. The repression that both men and women have faced has created it, and when the violence gets directed towards women, it's a distorted expression of what's been denied in us.

The feminine IS wild. The wild, even violent and destructive aspect of the feminine is what most men (and many women) most fear. Like our sexual energy, this wildness cannot be simply "turned off" when we are afraid of it. It has to go somewhere.

Our wildness can make us seem crazy or feel crazy-- when we don't own it and direct it appropriately. Just as women want to heal and love men, men want to heal and love women. In fact, it can be a compulsion.

A highly attuned lover knows exactly what his or her partner needs and offers that energy. Within any close relationship, we often unconsciously express each other's denied aspects for the sake of healing them.

On a collective level, this same phenomenon occurs. And for the most part, the wild and destructive feminine energy has not been considered "ok." The masculine has had more cultural permission to be rough or angry. So, the collective masculine (and I don't mean everyone all the time) has expressed violence towards the feminine.

Like a skilled and sensitive lover, the masculine naturally feels into the untapped wild feminine—and so expresses it on her behalf. Are war, rape, murder, or abuse acceptable ways to evoke this repressed energy? Of course not. But they show us how far off-balance we are.

I wonder… if the feminine rage, wrath, and moods were honored, would the masculine violence on earth would continue as it has? My guess is no.

And I think we are hitting this tipping point now, with a seeming increase in earthquakes, floods, and crazy weather. Gaia is speaking. Mother Earth won't be quiet and meek anymore.

May we realize these lessons and make friends with the wildness! By allowing this aspect of the feminine, it doesn't need to create harm. We can sit and enjoy it, knowing each wave relaxes back out to sea.

PRACTICE: *Freeing Your Wild Side*

- *Sit or stand with your feet flat on the floor and close your eyes.*
- *As you exhale, wiggle your hips and imagine a giant waterfall connecting the base of your body to the earth. Notice this waterfall draining away the stuck feelings you've been holding. Decide to release more of what's been holding you back from being your full, wild, dynamic feminine self.*
- *If you are standing, you might circle your hips, rock your pelvis, or jump rapidly up and down. You may make noises or exhale loudly.*
- *When you're ready, come to stillness and imagine a giant rose a few feet out in front of you. See it in full bloom, facing you. Imagine this rose as a vacuum that begins to draw more of this stuck energy out of you. Move the rose up and down, in front or in back of you, as needed.*
- *This stuff can feel serious! So, try out a state of wonder. For example, inquire if there's any repression you took on from your culture, family, or church. Ask to release these energies one by one. Get curious and notice what you feel as you go. Did you learn to hold back as a baby or small child, adolescent or young adult? Who taught you? What pictures have you been holding? Which life stories made you the way you were today? Were you impacted by past relationships? Ancestors? Past lives? Take at least a few breaths into each of these questions, as you allow any related energies to be vacuumed into your rose.*
- *As you release energy, you might yawn, get tired, or teary-eyed. Some people feel hot, cold, tingly, or have other physical sensations. If you're visual, you might "see" the rose change color, or even receive specific pictures of people or scenes. Some of us hear messages or an inner voice, and others just know what's releasing. Observe what comes up for you.*
- *If you're standing, you might continue moving your body as you*

feel guided, or even make sounds to help you release energy.

• *Once you're done, imagine what your fully dynamic feminine self would look like. What would she be, do, and feel? Is there a color or symbol which represents her best?*

• *Create a giant golden sun a few feet above your head, at least three times as big as your physical body. Put a magnet in the sun and allow it to draw your wildness, your fullness, and all that you are back to you. You don't need to know where it's coming from, but you can get curious. I always include other people and places, future and past. As you call your energy back, call back the pure life force and power you'd abandoned. See it all coming back to you as rays of golden light. In addition, sense your dynamic feminine self taking form as your gold sun. Let it emanate the full range of all that you are.*

• *Then allow it to pour through your entire body from head to toe, saturating every cell and filling every place you released energy. See yourself overflowing with gold, surrounded with a gold bubble of light as you open your eyes.*

UNRAVELING OUR PERPETRATOR AND VICTIM ROLES

I met a woman who claimed her husband was abusive. At first, I empathized with her story as any fellow mother would.

Then I got to know this new friend better. She was full of complaints and demands, and constantly focused on things that needed to be fixed. It was to the point of neurosis; to her, the world was unsafe, she was a victim and therefore felt compelled to speak— or even lash out—every time an "unsafe" situation arose.

It wasn't just her husband. After personally being the target of her "safety concerns," I learned that eight to nine others in the community had had similar challenges with her. I'd met her husband once, and he didn't seem "abusive" to me. One mutual friend said he was "normal."

In my dealings with her, I felt harassed by her constant threats and complaints. I bent over backwards trying to make things right, and I received almost no appreciation. By then, it struck me that she was actually the abusive one in her marriage.

Many years ago, I went to a relationship workshop with several hundred attendees. With the goal of increasing intimacy between men and women, we talked about the common feminine habit of nagging and complaining.

The facilitator asked, "How many of you guys would rather she just punch you in the face?"

Half the hands in the room went up. I don't recall a single man who didn't raise his hand.

It was eye-opening for me because, growing up, my dad was pegged as the perpetrator as my mom played the victim. I bought that story, too, until I was thirty-something and I had a heart-felt talk with my dad. As a kid, I was with my mom most of the time, so it didn't occur to me until later that her story was not the only story.

Looking back, it was a disempowering one that's been common for many women.

We overlook the "energy" aspect of things when we simply blame men and condone women without looking deeper. On the surface, my dad was an angry drunk at times, but my mom was a control freak who rarely gave him any energetic space. One of my intuitive friends looked at the dynamics and said, "If I was married to her; I'd drink too."

Of course, some men yell, hit, or otherwise intimidate or hurt people. That's not ok. But when my former friend bombarded me with punishment and anxiety, that wasn't ok with me either. I could've healed faster from a punch in the face!

What is hidden is harder to heal, let alone see in the first place. It can be very damaging. I can see why many men abuse women because sometimes these women are abusing them—in less obvious ways. The world doesn't recognize the feminine kind of abuse, and the men feel trapped and go off in rage.

Unfortunately, some very kind women get abused too because those men carry rage unrelated to their partners. But there is always more to the story, and I have seen many cases like my mom and my friend.

PRACTICE: Finding Your Empowerment

Write down the times you remember feeling like a victim in your life. For each, notice if there was anything in you that allowed it to happen. Were you getting a hidden benefit from it, did you have subconscious beliefs that said it was expected or that you deserved it, or did it remind you of past experiences that needed to surface in order to heal? Did it offer an important lesson? Write down whatever comes to your awareness.

Then, if relevant, note some healthier ways to meet those needs in the future.

Notes

Part 8

HEALING YOUR
RELATIONSHIP WOUNDS

Part 8 – Introduction

Part 8 is all about healing—recognizing and releasing your unhelpful patterns and stories. Here's where we dive into your childhood and family history, old relationship wounds, and even past lives.

This is not the easiest stuff to look at, yet I believe what we resist persists. Our shadows control us until we shine the light on them, and then they become a non-issue. So, in the long run, it's less painless and quicker to face them. We can do so with lightness, clear eyes, and courage. And sometimes, we need support.

It's important to note that this book is not meant to replace the services of a capable and loving professional. You may need a live human to hold space for you, and you may need practices and treatment methods that are more embodied than we can cover here.

It is my intention to provide you with resources and experiential practices to aid in your self-healing process. Following Part 8, we'll get more into how to create what you desire. In order to do so, you may need to first clear some stuff out of the way.

Because romantic relationships activate so much love, they render us vulnerable to an equal amount of pain. Be compassionate with yourself and others. Your continuing to choose love will trump the pain. Your dedication to create consciously and overcome past hurts will bring grace and open doors.

HOW YOU UNCONSCIOUSLY REQUIRE THE BEHAVIOR YOU HATE

Unknowingly, I used to believe a story that said, "If I show all of me, I'll be rejected, punished, and left alone." Because of this assumption, I picked men who couldn't "have" me, then held back so I wouldn't get hurt. Repeatedly the guys rejected me, and I asked, "What did I do wrong?"

A healer I consulted told me I was asking the wrong questions. About my relationship choices, he said I was like a PhD trying to get a job washing dishes, and so no one would hire me. It took me years to get it! The truth was, I had been rejecting myself, and picking the guys who mirrored that. The Universe so lovingly gives us what we put out.

If you have low self-worth, it's common to attract a partner who treats you poorly. If you're afraid of commitment, you might find yourself in long-distance relationships or with people who aren't really available. Or if you fear your man is unfaithful and start stalking and controlling him, he may become unfaithful when he wasn't before.

In addition to our unconscious beliefs, our energetic agreements with others also play a role in relationship challenges. For example: I worked with a woman who had a foul mouth and serious health issues. Her family saw her as the one with the problems. When I tuned in intuitively, I realized she was expressing what the rest of them would not. They saw anger as unacceptable and took great pride in being "civil" and balanced, even when they faced conflict. They meant well but were not honest, and that conflict had to go somewhere! Unknowingly, she took it on. Many families have a "family healer" like this. It would be much easier if each person just owned their own stuff!

Commonly, one partner in a relationship doesn't express certain emotions, which the other then over-expresses. For example, one never gets angry and the other one has a bad temper. The angry one gets blamed while the quiet one plays the victim or assumes superiority.

Especially when we're close, it's natural to feel and act out each other's stuff. We do it because we're unaware and because we love each other. But the effects are toxic. No one is free of emotions and no one is always positive. What keeps us happy, healthy, and in harmony with each other is to feel whatever we feel and find a constructive way to express it.

WHY RELATIONSHIP PATTERNS REPEAT

I was single, just out of a relationship with a Libra. As a friend and I looked back on what hadn't worked in that relationship, I remember her saying, "From now on, you won't waste your time with zodiac signs that you're not compatible with." (My sun sign is Capricorn, which is not traditionally compatible with Libra.) I laughed and we talked about which signs I'd be looking for next.

Within months, a new Libra man asked me out. I gracefully declined and kept imagining the conversation I would have with our mutual friend. "Feel free to set me up, but please NO Libras."

Another couple of months passed. I met someone new, felt the skies part, and the earth shake, then discovered his birthday. It was too late; I had to admit I liked yet another Libra. Why, why, why did this keep happening?

I realized that, besides my past partner, another two boyfriends (including my first one) plus my dad had sun and/or moon in Libra. Even though it wasn't what I thought I wanted, their energy felt familiar. It seemed that they had something to teach me, and that the Universe was trying to balance me somehow.

Whatever we say we don't want tends to chase us, so be careful. The subconscious only hears "yes."

When I realized I wanted to have a child, I was with a man who clearly did not. My desire grew to the point that this was a "must" for me, and the man and I started fighting a lot. In retrospect, I understand his anger. He hadn't bargained for this.

Night after night, we'd talk for hours with no solution. One morning over breakfast, we were fighting again, and I needed a break. I said I was going to yoga and he called me irresponsible. He claimed I was avoiding things, but I needed to clear and ground my energy. Clearly, talking so much wasn't fixing it, and I always felt better after yoga.

At the time, I also enjoyed listening to Krishna Das, whose music incorporated yoga mantras. I remember my partner saying, "If you were pregnant, I'd be telling you what to eat and what music to listen to." He particularly didn't like Krishna Das, who he said was "low energy and depressing."

Long story short, we split up. I moved to a new home, and soon after that, one of the band members for Krishna Das moved in next door. When I met his wife, she told me she was pregnant. Low energy and depressing? I don't think so. These were some of the happier, brighter people I'd met, and her pregnancy and birth seemed to go quite well.

My past partner started online dating, and he told me, "I don't know what's going on. All these yoga chicks want me."

What you resist persists. Releasing resistance takes courage. However, it's easier to heal your past and present than it is to do it over.

LEARNING TO HANDLE CONFLICT AND YOUR "INTIMACY THRESHOLD"

As soon as we get close or committed, our "intimacy threshold" can get triggered. This may look like "I don't know if I can stand so much love... This is beyond my comfort zone... What can I do to go back to what's familiar?" In these ways, we sabotage our relationships unknowingly.

Our hearts are only used to stretching open so wide. If we exchange more love or live with more passion, we can become afraid that we'll crack. So, when things get deep, we put the brakes on.

We don't mean to, not consciously, but our closure creeps up on us. Before we know it, we've been avoiding our partner for days. We've been finding excuses to be unavailable, to be distant. We've been keeping count in our heads of all the times he's done that annoying thing. We tell our girlfriends how hurt we feel.

Despite our irritation, we don't tell him. Even worse, we don't *show* him. The most toxic part is that we don't even let *ourselves* fully feel it. We've been talking, thinking our way around our feelings, and we think we're feeling them, but we're not.

Sometimes, we do things to provoke him to *be* the way we say we don't want him to be. We step in front of him as he's cleaning the kitchen. We get defensive and then blame him for accusing us. The fear in us wants to point the finger, wants "proof" that we have a real complaint, wants an excuse to distance.

There is a saying in Aikido that says, "The closer you are, the safer you are." Literally, in Aikido training, you might press your body against your partner's so you can *feel* where s/he is taking you. Then you can respond more effectively and keep yourself safer. By contrast, if you step a foot away, you lose touch with what's happening and are perfectly positioned to get punched in the face.

There's a time and place to have your own space within a relationship. If you're doing this so one or both of you can get clear and fill your own cups, wonderful. Unfortunately, if you're doing it to avoid conflict, it just makes things worse.

In the face of abuse, of course you need to protect yourself and I'm not recommending "staying close" if that's happening. Definitely remove yourself from the situation and get some help. When I say, "stay close," I'm talking about the daily conflict that most of us avoid. In my opinion, if we can get really good at facing this, we would have far less abuse. Tension wouldn't build up so much.

So often, I see women bagging on good men, and these men act differently when the women aren't around. Notice if you create distance and how that creates distance. What if you just inquired, just observed in those scary moments? What if you caught yourself the moment you hit your "intimacy threshold," the moment you felt so vulnerable and triggered that you wanted to run for the hills? What if you noticed that fear before the reaction happened, and then chose something else?

We often have to be in a lot of pain before we'll change these habits. Pain is a great motivator! And perhaps next time, let yourself be motivated by curiosity. "I wonder if I could feel more love?" "I wonder how I could provoke more closeness, or feel safe with the closeness I have?" Intimacy can feel more threatening than an argument. Pause and ask, "I wonder what I could do to get more of my needs met?" Notice your power there and let yourself be pleasantly surprised.

PRACTICE: *Affirmations to Clear Fears and Doubts*

On the left side of the worksheet that follows, write down the fears and doubts that come up for you in relationships. On the right side, write a corresponding positive belief for each.

For example, "I'm afraid he's going to cheat on me" turns into "I naturally attract a faithful partner, and I feel total trust in him and us." State your positive affirmations in present tense and use feeling-statements to add emotional power. These affirmations are about your experience, so using terms like "my partner" rather than someone's name (even if you have a partner) will keep you in integrity and open up more creative possibilities.

When you're done writing, record your affirmations on your phone or computer and listen to them regularly.

| *Fears and Doubts* | *Positive Beliefs* |

UNDERSTANDING YOUR KARMA AND CHILDHOOD STORY

Why do we fall in love with the people we fall in love with? Why do we end up in situations we wouldn't consciously choose?

Usually, they feel familiar because of our childhood stories. For example, if your father repressed his creativity to work and provide for the family, you might love artists and try to heal them. You might choose relationships where your own creativity gets stamped out. Guilt may come up if your partner provides for you (because subconsciously you don't want another man to suffer like your father did) so you marry a starving artist. We can beat our heads against the wall wondering why we keep repeating these patterns, and they're hard to shake, even when we recognize them.

As a conscious parent, it's helpful to know how this works. I was recently talking with a friend of mine whose son (just like my daughter) has a trustworthy, fully engaged father. She shared that certain little girls in their community seemed uncomfortable around men, in some cases including their own dads. Because my friend knew these girls' mothers, she knew that the mothers had each had painful experiences with men that had been passed on to the children. To their credit, this is not necessarily conscious or easy to resolve. However, there is a noted difference between kids whose parents have unhealed wounds and those who do not. We can be sensitive and appropriately protective without being overly guarded based on our own or other people's past.

Each of us has a story that goes farther back than we remember. I believe we've all lived many lifetimes, and that we pick our parents and life circumstances. We choose and "end up" in certain situations based on what we need to learn, contribute, or complete. For instance, a client of mine has had so many lifetimes being a monk, nun, or servant. She deeply desires to start a successful business but instead has lived her life as a "trash can" (her words), always putting other people's drama before her dreams. Because of this tendency to merge with others and put herself last, she's barely dated even though she is a loving and passionate soul!

Her path this lifetime has been to end her pattern so she can receive love and money and share her gifts. In the process, she's attracted partners who were addicts with poor boundaries, as well as family members and clients who've taken advantage of her. As painful as they were, these lessons pushed her to change her ways! Now she's attracting more support from the world around her because *she's* changed.

Whatever your story revolves around—rejection, abandonment, loss, control, feeling helpless, the need for security, unexpressed creativity etc.—I bet you've been working on it for lifetimes. You probably picked your family and relationships so far because they were the perfect triggers! It's not that we're gluttons for punishment, just that our souls don't mind the ride to healing and evolution. My teacher, Michael Tamura, used to say, "Karma is just God giving us another chance." It's such a relief to see it this way!

LETTING GO OF PAST RELATIONSHIPS

In order to attract a new relationship or move forward with the one you're in, it's important to heal from past relationships. If you have unprocessed anger, sadness, guilt, or other emotions—or if you're still energetically merged with a past partner—this will affect your love life going forward.

Healing occurs in waves. It takes time. You may feel fine about a past relationship for months, then hit an emotional dip where the grief overwhelms you. After it's over, you may finally get the clarity about what happened. With this can come remorse, anger, hurt, or a number of other things. There can be fear you're doomed to aloneness, and so you pick up the phone desperately hoping to get your past lover back—even when it was toxic.

All this is normal. You don't need to act on it but please acknowledge the influence of past relationships. The sooner you can feel it all (ideally with the help of a professional healer or counselor), the quicker it will pass. Once a guy I dated ended the relationship suddenly, three days after saying he was ready to move in together. I cried on the couch for a month and reached out for all the help I could find. Within two months, I was in a new relationship with a wonderful man who became my daughter's father.

You may not have time to cry on the couch for a month, or your feelings may be hard to access. That's ok too. Give yourself space. You may need to attend to work or family, or you may need a cycle of reclaiming and enjoying your life before you dive into the muck. Just notice if you feel tight and hardened or closed off to the world. This is a sign that your emotions have gotten stuck.

One of my clients had been divorced for nearly a decade. She dreamt of having another child with a new partner, but that window of opportunity came and went. Though she dated a bit, the only one she'd call a "boyfriend" had no money and erectile dysfunction. Otherwise, I'd get reports from her vacations, where she'd meet three men in a week. It felt like she was a huntress, seizing any moment to get even scraps, pushing these men to move forward instead of really allowing love into her life.

In repeated healing sessions, I found anger towards her ex-husband in her vaginal walls. She had demanded so much from him and felt she didn't receive enough. In their lovemaking, she was resentful and passive aggressive. Following her divorce, it's no wonder that she either approached sex as a "sport," or had a boyfriend that couldn't enter. Despite what she consciously desired, both of those options felt safer to her than attracting a truly available partner. As we cleared this energy, she softened, and much better prospects came her way.

If you're trying to process emotions and they feel like a bottomless pit, it may be a sign that you're holding onto someone else's energy. This could be energy from a past partner or a family member. Relationships can trigger patterns you learned from parents, so you may find you became just like your mom or your dad. If you suspect your emotions are stuck because they're not yours, I recommend re-visiting the meditation on "How to Feel Your Emotions and Release Those that Aren't Yours" from Part 6.

It's normal to hold a space in your heart for anyone you've loved deeply. There's a difference between holding the energy of the love you enjoyed and holding that specific person's energy. Sometimes, we know we need to release someone's energy. But until we honor the beautiful experiences we had together, we really don't want to. It may be a mixed bag. Even abusive relationships may have some goodness. This is why gratitude is important, along with discernment.

Here's what it might look like to affirm the goodness without holding a specific person's energy: "Thank you Universe, I loved the closeness and laughter I shared with _____. I release him/her now, and I welcome more of this feeling please, with a person who fully respects me."

PRACTICE: Releasing Past Lovers + Re-owning Your
Sexual Space

Besides the meditation we did in Part 6 to release emotions, I'd like to share a specific exercise to help you release past intimate partners and sexual energy from others.

- *Find a comfortable space to sit with your feet flat on the floor.*
- *Breathe. Feel yourself "land" in your body in present time.*
- *Create a grounding cord, such as a waterfall or tree trunk, from your hips down to the center of the earth. Exhale and allow yourself to release any stress down your grounding cord.*
- *One by one, ground your uterus and ovaries. Allow any foreign or stagnant energy to "drain" off of each of them, into the earth. This includes past partners, creative blocks, trauma around childbirth or conception, programming from others, etc.*
- *Imagine a fluffy, gold sticky rose a few feet out in front of you. See the rose like a vacuum and swish it through your sexual space, entire body, and energy field. Let this rose absorb any energy you no longer need—from someone who checked you out once to someone you slept with for decades.*
- *Clear sexual trauma by taking the rose to the amygdala gland at the base of the brain, to the tailbone/root chakra, and through the trance medium channels that run along left and right sides of your head and spine. These are places where we hold survival information, subconscious thoughts and feelings, and energy associated with spacing out (which is common in the case of trauma).*
- *When your healing feels complete for now, see the rose float out in front of you until it bursts into light at the edge of the horizon. Know that whatever energy you released will be neutralized and returned to wherever it came from.*

- *Create a gold sun above your head. Just as other people's energy has been in your space, consider that your energy has been with others' space. Specifically, let all your energy that's off with current or past partners or love interests be magnetized into the sun. See waves of gold light pouring in. Don't worry, they won't love you any less. In fact, you become more attractive when all your energy is with you, and others feel the space to go towards. Having your energy with a love interest can actually de-magnetize him. As for those you no longer wish to attract, just hold to your self-love and clarity, and you'll only attract those you're aligned with. So, call all your energy back.*

- *Once your sun is full to the brim, take a deep breath and "drink" the light in. From the crown of your head to the base of your spine, tips of your fingers and toes, and out beyond the edges of your skin, allow the golden light to radiate within and around you—3 feet above your head, below your feet, front and back, left and right. Especially fill in your sexual space and all the places that you cleared.*

- *When you're done, open your eyes and come out of meditation.*

HEALING YOUR LINEAGE

Most of the time when my client is really stuck, particularly with a health or relationship challenge, it goes back to something in their lineage. If we've done several sessions without noticeable change, this is where I go, and it's always powerful.

It's generally something they don't "know" about, perhaps many generations back, something the family didn't really talk about because it was shushed or shamed. If there was suicide, incest, abuse, addiction, or major trauma—it affects everyone in the family line, particularly because it got shoved into the closet. People's unexpressed and repressed feelings get passed on. If only we bring darkness to light, it ceases to control us and the generations to come.

One of my clients couldn't stop feeling inferior in the business she had with her husband. Identified as a feminist and with a husband who wanted her to shine, she couldn't figure out why she had this feeling. Immediately I saw her male ancestors, who were not so comfortable with feminine power. In spirit they showed me their fear of feminine energy (in women and in themselves), along with their shame and pain about repressing it. Because their energy was "in her" through her DNA and family story, she was acting it out unknowingly. We did a healing for them and for her, and then re-set her life as a businesswoman in "present time." She started to feel much more confident.

"Who's Myrtle?" I asked another woman who came to see me.

Without batting an eye, she told me that Myrtle was her grandmother who'd suffered some painful events. Because my client knew what Myrtle had been through, we were able to put 2 and 2 together and understand how that was impacting her current challenges.

PRACTICE: *Ancestral Clearing*

This is a meditation to heal your family line. You don't have to know of any past family trauma to benefit. I simply recommend considering what you could most use support with, in your life and relationships. Is there a repeating pattern or challenging situation you can't seem to change?

- *With your healing intention in mind, sit in a calm place with your feet flat on the floor, and close your eyes.*
- *Notice your breath moving in and out of your belly, heart, and chest. Decide to smoothly allow more breath in and more breath out.*
- *Create a tree trunk or waterfall from your hips and send it down to the center of the earth. Exhale as you relax and "land" more fully in your body, letting any stuck emotions or energy release down this grounding cord.*
- *In your mind's eye, visualize two golden lines of light beginning a few feet in front of you. See one on the left and one on the right, each of them extending out as far as you can imagine. The one on the left represents your mother's family line, and the one on the right represents your father's. Imagine these ancestral lines like tree branches. I suggest using your birth mother and father (even if you don't know those people) because their DNA comprises your body.*
- *Wherever you see dark spots within these gold lines, there is some "shadow" event or energy that needs healing. Notice if you see more of these on your father's side, mother's side, or they're in both fairly evenly. Do you sense more darkness towards the front of the lines (more recent?) or towards the back (longer ago?). You may get pictures, symbols, or other messages about what occurred. You might feel emotions or sensations, without specifically knowing what happened. That's ok. Breathe and be with whatever is arising,*

letting your grounding support you.

• *When you're ready, you can cleanse each family line by imagining two golden roses in full bloom. Run one rose through your mother's line and one through your father's line. Imagine these roses have a vacuum action, clearing the darkness and restoring the light to your ancestors. I think of this as a blast of love and forgiveness. When you feel complete with this, send the roses off to the edge of the horizon and see them go "poof" into bursts of pure light. Then, dissolve the ancestral lines in your minds' eye, and come out of meditation.*

• *Over the days and weeks to come, pay attention to any changes in the situation you desired healing on. If needed, come back to this meditation as often as you'd like.*

OVERCOMING JEALOUSY

Jealousy is a big one that nearly every woman faces from time to time. The "other woman" is like the "boogey man" passed on for centuries, always threatening your love and security. She won't seem to go away, no matter your situation. For example:

- You like a guy and want him to be yours, and so feel threatened by every attractive woman around him.
- The guy you're attracted to is another relationship.
- You're dating someone who's "not ready" to settle down.
- You're in a committed relationship but are always wondering who he's looking at or what he's doing.

Becoming exclusive, getting engaged, or moving into marriage will not cure jealousy. Only loving yourself fully will. And from there, of course, choosing a trustworthy partner is necessary.

Jealousy, like all emotions, is not "bad." Like all emotions, it has a message for us and, in this case, it's about something we've disowned or disallowed ourselves. You can be a confident woman in a secure relationship, have a pang of jealousy, and think, "Wow—I guess I need to let myself have what she's having. I guess I need to own my beauty / sassiness / sexiness / success (insert name of quality you see in her). And then use that feeling as fuel to get really clear and become more of yourself.

The other important cure for jealousy is to remember the Divine plan. From the ego's limited point of view, there may be a shortage of "good men." It's easy to convince yourself that there has to be a winner and a loser. However, from a higher perspective, everything and everyone has their place. Life is always giving.

Translated into "real life," the "other woman" may be protecting you from having a partner who wouldn't be good for you. I've talked to countless women who, years after a painful breakup, said, "Thank

God I got out of that situation. I've got something so much better now."

If he *is* or *will be* your man, another woman can actually be an important catalyst for many possible reasons. She may be showing him how great you are by her being everything he doesn't want. If he's dating her, she's likely an easier place for him to practice having a healthy relationship, so he's fully ready when he gets to you. If he's non-committal in dating you, his desire to "play the field" now might keep him from having a mid-life crisis when your kids are teenagers. If you're married, his attractive co-worker might give him a feeling of success that he brings home to you—in the bedroom and in the pocketbook. And, as I mentioned, whatever you see in that "other woman" is a great reminder of what you want to be and have.

Men aren't wired for monogamy as we are, so we might do well to accept him looking at other women, or even having crushes. All this is normal and indicates a healthy libido—that he then shares with you. This is where we also need to pick partners evolved enough to control themselves. It's really about re-directing the energy back to your relationship. How you and your partner do that depends on your comfort levels. Some women even go to strip clubs or watch porn with their partners, in order to learn what he likes and so he doesn't have to hide those desires away from her. At whatever level you do it, this type of thing can add a new level of excitement and a boost in intimacy for both of you!

FORGIVENESS

Forgiveness is a tricky one. People don't want to do it because they still hurt. It's hard to let go and they don't want to condone—or perhaps even accept—what happened.

Michael Tamura had a different take. He called it "for giving." With this definition, forgiveness doesn't require agreeing with or even understanding another person or event. It simply means to choose a giving attitude. Punishing or judging someone "takes" not only from them but also from yourself and all life. Even while honoring your pain, you can give to the one who "did it to you" by wishing them well. Doing so silently is fine, if this makes the most sense for you.

At least, this practice helps you release your own charge and—at best—your blast of love can help them to change any inappropriate behavior. Contrary to our ego's idea, people change more when we remain neutral about them!

On a spiritual level, you can "give" things up to the Divine. If the unfathomable occurs—for instance if a partner dies, betrays you, or leaves suddenly—you may never understand. But it doesn't "give" to life when you stay frozen in shock. Feeling numb for a time is totally human. If you've experienced something like this—consider that even though you don't understand, at some point you can let go in service to further life.

You can also give to yourself by choosing more self-care, seeing healers, and praying for compassion. You can give to others by using your painful experiences to support them—from literally teaching what you've learned to simply being a loving presence. Don't underestimate the power of this.

PRACTICE: Forgiveness Prayers

Please adapt the following to your specific needs, using these or any other words that ring true to your heart. Speak them daily, and/or record and play them back to yourself daily.

General Forgiveness Prayer

Dear Spirit,

Please help me to release and forgive anyone who has ever harmed me, consciously or not, on any level, through all time. Please help others to release and forgive me for any way I have harmed them, on any level, through all time. Please help us all to release and forgive ourselves for any hurts or wrongs, conscious or not, on every level throughout all time. Thank you.

To Forgive a Specific Person or Situation

_____, *I now release and forgive you through all time for* _____, *and I see each of us and all concerned bathed in love, guided by light, living the greatest plan for our lives in grace with a giving spirit now and always. Amen.*

Part 9

UNLEASHING YOUR CREATIVE ENERGY

Part 9 – Introduction

Female creative energy is hugely powerful and hugely misunderstood. It's been both revered and denied in our culture. It is the source of all life, and try as you might, you can't shut it off.

Allow it fully and it makes a baby, a business, or beautiful home. With less consciousness, you talk, shop, or organize. Push it down and it's easy to end up sick, depressed, or neurotic.

This force within you is both irresistibly attractive and totally overwhelming to most men. The key is in how you direct it. In Part 9, you'll receive practical tips on how to use your creative energy successfully, particularly in your romantic relationships.

Freeing your creativity erodes worries and doubts. Finding trust in it dissolves tightness. Knowing how to use it unkinks the knots in your heart.

UNDERSTAND HOW YOUR CREATIVE ENERGY AFFECTS HIM

We women have the incredible power to create life in our bodies. Whether or not we've had children, have had a hysterectomy, or are in menopause, that wiring is still there.

This is why we start planning our future on the first date with a man we like. Our female creative energy thinks in time spans of 18 years. This *is* appropriate when making a baby. Without awareness, it's a programmed instinct that puts pressure on situations it shouldn't. Planning our future together on the first date, pushing for commitment or marriage or even revealing too much of ourselves in the early stages has been shown to drive men away.

Being vulnerable and honoring our desire to bond are beautiful things. However, cultivating our playfulness and taking our time is both more attractive and more honoring of our value. So, I recommend trying to stay in the moment more often, at least when you're with him.

Besides making babies, we can use this energy for many things. Our 140 watts of power needs to go somewhere. Creative projects, cooking, gardening, or starting a business can be great outlets.

If we aren't using our feminine creativity constructively, it expresses any way it can. Girlfriends chatting 100 miles an hour is one common example. A more toxic and equally common occurrence is when we make a man our project. Whether that means healing or coaching him, obsessing over how to "get" him, or constantly correcting him and managing his behavior, it overwhelms him and keeps us in a cycle of frustration.

Making a baby requires perfection. If we put the eyeball where the kneecap goes, that would be a big problem. Men, however, are human and by nature imperfect. Life is imperfect. So, nagging him because he's 5 minutes late, telling him how to run his business, or analyzing how his mother issues are affecting your marriage doesn't tend to bring such great results.

PRACTICE: Balancing Your Female Creative Energy

• *Find a comfortable space to sit with your feet flat on the floor.*

• *Close your eyes, notice your breathing, and bring your attention to your body and this moment.*

• *Ground yourself by visualizing a tree trunk or waterfall from your hips to the center of the earth.*

• *A few feet out in front of your belly, imagine a ball of light made of colors and energetic patterns. This is your female creative matrix, the psychic equivalent of your womb.*

• *Now ground this ball of energy. See a light beam connecting it to the center of the earth. This grounding allows you to release any invalidation, any programming, or other people's energy that's been affecting your creativity. You might see your ball get brighter, you may see pictures of what's releasing, or you might just feel or know things as this happens.*

• *Look at your female creative matrix and see what colors are starting to emerge. Ask yourself: "If my creativity was fully expressed, what color would it be today?" Let that color grow brighter and stronger.*

• *Now bring some of your female creative energy to the top of your head. This balances things out and aligns your immense creativity with your soul's purpose.*

• *When you're ready, open your eyes and come out of meditation.*

MYTHS OF THE FEMININE: THE FEMININE IS PASSIVE

Imagine for a moment that you're a man walking into a room full of women. Do you think you'd be most attracted to the quietest, most perfectly dressed woman who seems bored—or to the one who's smiling, laughing, brightly dressed and glancing your way?

Men like to conquer but at the same time they don't want to work so hard to find you. Most of them work hard enough during the day. And by "you," I don't mean your body, I mean your radiant energy. This is where your creative energy works in your favor. That 140 watts of energy is irresistible *if it's not directed towards him.*

Translation: This isn't about chasing him across the room, it's just about enjoying yourself and appearing available. If you're feeling good, he'll be attracted. It's a win-win because what attracts him most is your pleasure.

It's easy to say and the effects are obvious but what trips some women up is the feeling that maybe pleasure is not ok, that they don't deserve it, or that this is too easy. Part of being feminine is letting yourself be and receive. So yes, it IS easy, and yes it works even in a committed relationship.

Sometimes this is especially important once you've been together a long while, and you've long stopped dressing up for dates or getting excited every time you see each other. In this case, ask yourself what makes you feel alive, and allow yourself to enjoy whatever that is. Your partner will notice and love you for it!

MYTHS OF THE FEMININE: THE FEMININE CAN NEVER SPEAK FIRST

Over and over I see this in my clients. Whether it's in dating situations or long-term relationships, women have been afraid that speaking up is either unsafe or will make them seem too masculine. And it's not true. Being feminine includes immense creativity, and to repress it does a dis-service to everyone. The trick is in how we express it, especially with men.

Once I had a crush on a man for several years. Sometimes we'd flirt, I'd feel such strong chemistry and was sure we'd be dating soon. I kept waiting for him to make a move, but nothing happened.

Finally, I reached a point where I thought I was over it. I was weeks away from moving out of state when he had a serious injury. Suddenly I was sleepless and crying, feeling his pain, thinking I'd never see him again. As it turns out, I got to see him once before I left. I had to share how I felt!

Heart fluttering, I said, "I always thought one day I'd get to know you better, and then I thought I'd never see you again, so it's such a gift to see you today." And I went on to describe many things I've admired about him over the years. He smiled, obviously touched and said, "Well, keep in touch." We had about four big hugs within 30 minutes.

As I drove through the desert towards my new home days later, I felt like my heart was bursting out of my chest. For days. I'd had no agenda, just a pure desire to share, to not miss an opportunity to love. And his openness was a powerful teaching for me.

If I had shared sooner, who knows what might have happened? Maybe he hadn't been interested or available to have a relationship with me. But meanwhile, I realized how much creative energy I'd put into wondering, into the lie of rejection. Regardless, I trust the timing of the conversation and am infinitely grateful for knowing him and for the evolution it brought me.

This helped me re-write the rules I learned from my passive mother and some old-fashioned relationship coaches. Previously, I believed if men didn't contact me first, they either weren't available, or they weren't strong enough men. I also feared speaking first because I didn't want to be the "man" in the relationship.

While I think aspects of that philosophy are valid, I feel sad when I realize how limiting it can be. I wish I hadn't had such rigid ideas about being pursued. Some men are just shy, or given a number of women to choose from, they want to put their energy where they feel they have a chance. They need a little invitation.

It's one thing to chase a man, and it's another thing to smile, ask him about himself, or share your feelings in his presence. Looking back, I remember how many intuitive friends suggested I express myself to my friend during that last year we lived in the same town. My favorite line came from my male chiropractor, who told me to say, "If you asked me out, I'd say yes."

"Men are lazy," he said. "They need a little help."

INVITE HIM

The masculine doesn't like to be told what to do, how to be, or what to think. However, there are ways to invite him. You'll have better results with less work.

Have you ever ranted for hours to your girlfriends about your partner's shortcomings, or about the inadequacies of men you meet? What if there was a way to re-direct all that energy into actually evoking something else from a man? There is, and that way is your art.

It's like the old trick of dropping a handkerchief, or wearing high heels so you appear vulnerable, but you don't have to take it that far. With a subtle change in your posture, he'll open the door for you. Seeing your show of enthusiasm about a certain movie, he'll take you to see it. Hearing your simple request for help, he'll happily share all he knows.

You know it deep in your bones, but you may have to be the first of your girlfriends or family to dare to do it. Your guy may never have seen it before, so be patient, then watch the magic happen.

How comfortable are you in receiving? Does it feel safer to just take care of yourself and not "need" anything from a man? We are all whole within but are you willing to let go and expand into more than you can be on your own?

Truly, the masculine is energized when he gives to you. If you have walls up, he'll go next door. And yes, he'll go to a less attractive, less successful, meaner woman if her heart is open more than yours. Men may seem dense, but they feel this even if they can't explain it. That's why you might scream at God knowing you're the total package but keep getting passed by. Believe me, I've been there.

Unfortunately, closing down in frustration generally means you'll get less prospects. With a conscious partner or on your own, though, clean anger expressed in the moment can create breakthroughs. You don't need to avoid it or any other emotion, just stay connected in the moment and don't vent or project. If you have bottled up emotions that keep affecting your current relationships, then work on releasing them on your own or with a trusted professional.

Ask questions. You push a man away by constantly chattering (easy for the feminine especially when we're nervous) but you *invite* him in by being genuinely curious. Engage him and he'll be delighted and feel seen and valued. Then he may be the one talking non-stop!

PRACTICE: Express More!

Get out your pen and explore how you could express more with the man or men in your life. Maybe it's about having more fun with your wardrobe or sharing your feelings more openly. If you're single, try smiling and holding eye contact longer, or letting that special someone know how much he inspires you. In a committed relationship, instead of changing or coaching your partner, perhaps use that creative energy for something else that brightens your day. He just might notice! What are your ideas? Write them down now.

Notes

GIVE ENERGY BUT NOT DIRECTION

Let's say you want to change a man. Maybe you want your love interest to make a move. What if your husband or boyfriend has some annoying habits that you think would be easy to fix?

How do you influence him without emasculating him, pissing him off, or making him feel like an idiot? Believe me, men are sensitive, and this is easy to do!

Give energy but not direction. Pretend you're dancing and let him lead—but know he can't lead if you're stiff, or if you're floppy and lifeless.

How this might translate is this… Let's say he asks you out to a movie you have no interest in but you're very excited to get to know him. Do you go anyway and pretend you like it? Do you say no with no reason, or make a face?

What if you said something like "I'd love to go out with you but last time I watched a violent movie I couldn't sleep all night." Then he feels your interest and doesn't feel criticized. He knows something more about you and how to please you. All in one simple sentence. You don't have to take it any further, just stop there and see what he does.

You've just left the ball in his court. If he wants you and not just a companion to see that movie with, he'll try something else. Men love a creative challenge. If he's not really that interested or if he can't think up anything else to offer, that's helpful for you to know early.

So many women assume men are idiots, when really, they just need cues from us. It's one thing to want him to take charge; but waiting for him to read your mind is grandma-programming!

Some women might go on to ask the man to do something else. This may be ok here and there, but it *does* put you in the masculine role. It means you may not find out how interested he really is, and it doesn't give him the opportunity to be his Divine Masculine self.

SENSUALITY

We can get so fixated on being the "perfect" woman we think he wants. If only we said all the right things, never had body hair or bad breath, and wore all the trendiest outfits, we'd be assured of his love! Heck, you might even try to perfect your "energy" by following everything in this book. Ha! Thank Goodness, it isn't that hard.

Well, for some of us, what I'm about to share will be harder: *Get sensual.* If it's easy for you, great. Go ahead and enjoy!

For many women, sensuality can be uncomfortable for various reasons—anything from religious programming to serious trauma. If so, start slow and give yourself extra TLC. Take one baby step and see how you feel before moving on. You may need a few deep breaths; or you may need days or weeks before reading more. Practicing regular meditation and energy clearing is super important. If you're getting stuck on your own, I highly recommend finding a healer or counselor, or taking a yoga or dance class.

Ready to dive in? Ok! Sensuality is not about how your body looks. I'm sure you've seen women of all shapes and sizes with great sex appeal. When a woman feels good about herself, she moves in a delicious way. Her pleasure draws you in... who wouldn't want to experience it? Her sighs, her gestures, the way she looks at you are all magnetic.

Sensuality is not necessarily about sex. If you're struggling to feel attractive, take a slow bite into some melty chocolate. Turn on your favorite music and sway. Take a bubble bath. Stroke your wrists or your neck when your workday gets dull.

Do these things when no one's looking. Do them for yourself. Your effort to be sexy is NOT sexy. Your pleasurable flow that someone might accidentally walk in on is super sexy. It's one of your feminine gifts.

PLAYFULNESS

Playfulness is your secret weapon. Playfulness attracts friends and partners. Playfulness helps you through a dating challenge or marital crisis. Playfulness creates a feeling of safety. It's great medicine for our overly serious world.

Once I liked a guy that I worked with. He told me he felt it too but couldn't date me due to professional boundaries. Intuitively, I sensed he was guarded for other reasons. I could have poked and prodded, cried and begged, or analyzed and coached him. Instead, I warmly shared everything from my hurt feelings to deep respect to excited passion. I joked a bit and at the right moment, I gently inquired about what I was sensing and confirmed my hunch. He admitted that he'd been avoiding relationships due to past heartbreak.

I said, "I want to blast your walls down."

He cracked a smile and said, "They're pretty thick, aren't they."

Playfulness can be hard to access unless you have a spiritual perspective. I had to cry for days, pray a lot, and enlist the help of friends to get ready for the above conversation. When things don't go your way, remembering that there's a bigger picture provides huge relief. If it seems like you're flailing in the dark, this perspective is the crack that lets the light in.

Sometimes spirituality is approached with reverence but all the spiritual masters I've ever witnessed are very funny! We can have both immense respect and immense irreverence—for God, for love, and for life.

From a healing perspective, the only "danger-zone" is when energy gets stuck. As long as we're feeling our feelings, expressing ourselves, and facing what life gives us—we can handle the pain and inevitable growth that comes with being human.

Once we've felt it all, what's left is freedom. Once we've forgiven, what's left is laughter. Only when we stop taking things too seriously, do we have perspective and spaciousness. From this place we attract and create with virtually no effort. It takes work but it's not the work we generally think we need to do.

EXPRESSING ARTFULLY

How do you know when to express, and when to relax and receive? And when you do express, how do you know what's "too much" or "too little"? It's a fine line, and the keys are:

- **Sensitivity.** As we discussed in Part 2, your feminine receptivity is a gift. It will allow you to sense whether he's open to you, and if so, what to say and when to say it. Sometimes your timing, or a subtle tweak in your tone or language makes all the difference!

- **Playfulness**. If you're serious and stuck, any little thing you share sounds heavy. When your energy is light and detached, knowing that there's a bigger picture, you can easily express deeper thoughts and feelings. He relaxes and he hears more.

- **Feeling messages**. He can dismiss your ideas and resist your advice. But he'll listen when you share your own feelings without analysis, especially when they're located in your body. If you say, "I get a warm feeling all over me when you talk about that," how can he argue? This approach has so many benefits! You get more in touch with yourself, you get heard, and he relaxes. And for a man who has trouble accessing his feelings, you just modeled for him how to do so. He feels safer to feel and share when you go first, and especially when you don't try to coach him or evaluate him.

HOLDING BACK & OVEREXTENDING GO TOGETHER

Most of us women do either "too much" or "too little," applying our efforts in the wrong direction. The programming that says the feminine is passive causes us to hold back our desires, our feelings, and our creativity. The stuck feeling makes us really, really serious. Holding back causes us to either explode or implode. One or the other is inevitable.

It's particularly a problem when we express our feelings after the fact. This is where women get the reputation of being crazy. Months or years after he pissed you off, your angry outburst or sudden tears do seem nuts. He has no context for them when you're in the middle of a stroll through the park. You seem unsafe. He doesn't feel he can trust you and he certainly doesn't want to chance bringing you around his friends and family. You think your emotions are the problem and you feel uncomfortable around him, them, or both. Then you become more volatile, more bottled up, and the whole thing spirals downhill really fast. Good luck getting out of this one!

Your emotions were never the problem. Assuming they're *your* emotions (see the exercise, "*How to Feel Your Emotions and Release Those That Aren't Yours*" from Part 6), the main problem is timing. Yell at him when he steps on your toe or cry when he forgets your anniversary, and he'll get it. Any man who cares about you won't want to see you upset, and if he knows why, he'll want to fix it. You get what you want, and he feels relieved that he can do something.

It's known that most men like a woman who's "low maintenance," but consider that your authenticity is actually easier than you pretending to be "nice" constantly. Being happy all the time is not normal, and therefore it's not trustable. Of course, if you get triggered during a business meeting or in front of your kids, you may need to bring it up later—but don't wait too long. Respond genuinely in each moment and he relaxes, knowing where he stands.

Another reason we might hold back then overdo it later is if we've fallen into the belief that we're powerless as women. Playing an overly passive role due to our programming, we allow things to happen that we wouldn't have chosen. Assuming we can't or shouldn't rock the boat, we go with the flow and then overcompensate once we realize we don't like what's happening. This can show up in subtle ways, such as not speaking up in a conversation, then becoming controlling or passive-aggressive. At more extreme levels, it can lead to breakups or domestic violence. Again, the keys are listening to your senses, detaching through spiritual focus and playfulness, and expressing things early before they build up.

Another time we overextend is when feminine vulnerability feels unfamiliar. It wasn't modeled to us. For those of us that grew up in the age of feminism, we tend towards acting strong, leaning into our inner masculine in the name of equality. And so, we "do" and "think" and "achieve" more than our feminine selves want to. To soften and receive feels out of control. We don't want to get trapped like our grandmothers. We aren't sure if today's men will step up. These are valid concerns, and yet we can lead the way.

AS A WOMAN, YOU ARE MEANT TO LEAD

The river shapes the riverbank. As women, our energy and creativity become the guiding light in a man's world. Yes, he has his own purpose independent of us, and he needs to have that. Consider though that you're fuel for that purpose. You teach, lead, and inspire any man who gets close to you, and you even guide the masculine energy on the planet.

We are leaders because we have the power to create life, along with the spiritual and practical gifts that come with this. We lead from our hearts, not from reason or action. These things have a place. But just as the riverbank serves the river, they must serve the heart in order to be in balance.

Your heart is the wellspring from which you give your creative gifts, your love and purpose. Your heart knows your truth and feels your way through every situation. It is the point of balance between your mind and your body, and it harmonizes your various needs as well as those of others. Here, you have the gift of compassion, which means "with passion." Compassion is not a boring state of peace!

In recent times, many people have confused feminine leadership with women acting like men. In part because of all our cultural distortions, some men express more feminine qualities than some women. It's lovely how the Divine Feminine is waking up in all of us! And for those of us with female bodies, may we wake up to the leadership qualities we innately have!

It's the feminine that considers how people are feeling, that sees interconnectedness and has the intuitive vision to steer things in positive direction. It is our unconditional love that helps others feel valued and safe, and our creativity which brings new solutions.

May we offer these natural gifts freely, all while celebrating the masculine-- just as the river celebrates the riverbank.

PRACTICE: *Activating Your Heart's Leadership*

- *For this one, I recommend standing with your feet flat on the floor.*

- *Relax your body, drop down into your hips, and send a grounding cord down from there into the center of the earth.*

- *Soften your belly. Soften your heart.*

- *Begin to sway your arms side to side, up and down.*

- *Take your right hand to your left shoulder and swipe your hand all the way down to the tips of your left fingers. Repeat on the inside and outside of each arm.*

- *Rub your hands together until you feel a tingle between your palms.*

- *Your arms and hands are channels for your heart's expression as well as your voice and creativity. Shake your hands over your head as you enjoy the feeling of more energy flowing through these channels.*

- *Ask your heart what it would like to share now. Are some of your gifts ungiven? Are there ways you could express more love? Have you been holding back your creativity or passion? If so and you started to share more, what would that look like? Take all the time you need to observe your heart's yearnings.*

- *Next, feel with your heart into the heart of someone you love. If there's no one in particular, feel into the world or some segment of the world. What is this person or group feeling? What are they needing? Don't take these feelings into your body, just sense with your heart.*

- *Considering both your gifts and others' needs, ask your heart if there are ways you could lead more effectively. Listen and observe for as long as you'd like, then come out of meditation.*

Part 10

TAKING RESPONSIBILITY

Part 10 – Introduction

We women are naturally responsible. Since we are wired to make babies, it's instinctive in us. Misapplied, it's common for us to assume responsibility for things that aren't ours. This can cause a lot of pain and psychic confusion.

Getting caught up in the "mother" archetype, past trauma, and cultural wounds around masculine-feminine dynamics may contribute to this. Sometimes we fear we won't get what we want, and it's hard to relax and receive. Then we become hyper-functional as if to assure it.

On the other hand, stuck in the feminine distortion of neediness, we project responsibility elsewhere. "He did it to me." "If only I could find the right guy, or if only he'd do what I want—all my problems would be solved." We try to seduce, or we do nothing, feeling helpless. That's not it either!

Part 10 gives you tools to boost your confidence by becoming responsible for yourself and your happiness. It teaches you artfulness rather than coercion. It releases you from the binds of all the things you thought you had to fix that you just don't!

Ready?

WHAT IS HEALTHY RESPONSIBILITY?

I used to sell a "Loving Relationship" flower essence blend at holistic expos. It was amusing how often women would point to it and say, "I don't need this, but my husband does!" Of course, if they didn't need healing, they wouldn't be complaining about men. When I get clients like this, I help them find their power by seeing what *they* can shift (energetically or physically) to improve their relationships.

Often, my client thinks her man is causing the problem and completely misses what she's doing to contribute to it. In other cases, she has become her mother or his mother, and she is living out a story that doesn't apply to now. Sometimes, she responds to things through the lens of all the past hurts she never fully felt. Her husband might deeply love her. However, she blames him because the way he shows it reminds her of the way her father disappointed her. Responsibility in these cases means being self-aware enough to see the current situation clearly.

Responsibility sounds so serious! Taken literally, it simply means *the ability to respond.* When you fully inhabit your feelings and body, you will be able to respond based on what feels good or bad to you. From an embodied place, you'll see clearly. And then, you'll simply require everything in your world to line up with your self-love. Something (whether a behavior or a whole relationship) that doesn't match this love will just be obvious.

You can say, "Yes, please," or "No, thank you," as the lady you are and stay soft and open. You can simply move in the direction of what pleases you and express yourself as you feel your way into different possibilities. When you get really good at this, you don't get very far down the wrong road before your body says "stop." And here, there is no drama.

You can use more "I" statements in conversation and do your best to avoid blame. For example, "You never do the dishes" might cause him to do the dishes but, in succumbing, he'll feel like a little boy who got in trouble. Saying something like "I've had such a long day, and the idea of doing dishes exhausts me" allows him to step up as a man proud to make you happy. The result is totally different!

It can be scary to take your attention off of his behavior and focus on yourself. But he'll feel such relief that you aren't fixing or coaching him, and he'll finally relax when your words and actions line up with his sense of where you're at. Even when you feel guilty or scared that you're not doing what he seems to want, you might be surprised at how your self-care will draw him towards you.

Sometimes this looks dramatic. For example, if a man is not committing, you may have to leave or date other men even though you really want *him*. With a man who's controlling or if you've lost yourself in your support role, you might start a job or creative project.

Healthy responsibility includes trusting that life is bigger than your current circumstances. Know that the love you crave is "out there" as well as within you. When you really believe this, the right man will feel honored to be with you. You'll never 100% please anyone on a personality level, and that's ok.

WHAT IS TOXIC RESPONSIBILITY?

If you try ignoring your feelings, they'll only get stronger. He'll feel the disconnect between where you're at and how you show up. You'll know something's wrong, but you won't know what, so you'll do what's culturally acceptable—that is, look outside yourself and try to fix something "out there." And if that means him, he'll really start to fuss. Now you'll have even more to process. But because you can never solve his stuff for him and because only you can solve your own, it will be a tangled-up, never-ending maze.

With my college boyfriend, I ended up taking responsibility for every issue that came up. I felt like I was in a "good relationship" because we had so much in common and we talked a lot. It took me years to realize I was always taking the blame, trying to fix whatever issues arose.

It felt so "normal" to do it that way. That's how I did it with my dad. That's what I saw women doing everywhere—but it's disempowering to everyone involved.

Besides being overly accommodating when they're late or don't follow through with something, and besides always being the one to patch up an argument, your taking toxic responsibility can happen energetically. For example, let's say your partner had a rough childhood where his father talked down to his mother. Maybe his mother was a control freak. All of a sudden, he starts criticizing you, and you anxiously monitor his every move. If you didn't have those patterns in past relationships, you've likely absorbed his issues and are acting them out.

Taking responsibility for something like this is like entering a black hole. Being aware, releasing what's not yours, and relating to each other with compassion will yield much better results.

PRACTICE: *Are You Appropriately Responsible?*

How could you take more healthy responsibility? Are there ways you're taking toxic responsibility?

Notes

WHEN HIS ENERGY MAKES YOU FEEL HEAVY

Focusing on him rather than yourself can make you feel "heavy" quite quickly! Now, taking on *anyone's* energy besides your own is confusing. But for a woman, taking on a man's energy can literally cause weight gain!

Neither feminine nor masculine energy is better or worse, as there's a need for both in the world. But try running 40 watts of energy (his) through a 140-watt body (yours) and see how you feel. At times like this, your natural zing feels enveloped in sludge. Your energy feels "thick" and your thoughts and body slow down. "Ugh. What's wrong?" you think. It's easy to get depressed.

Healing him, or serving his *need* at your own expense, comes at a high price. It doesn't even work, because he's not attracted to you when your energy is just like his. Especially when he's in a rough space! In these moments he needs your light. Dance, fill your own cup, and let him see it without pouring it into him.

On this note, simply being together all the time can cause a depolarization of energy between you and your man. This is where some older couples even start to look alike. The romantic fantasy of being "inseparable" isn't as romantic as it seems.

PRACTICE: How to Heal Any Relationship by Separating Your Energies

- *Sit down with your feet flat on the floor and close your eyes.*
- *Begin to notice your breathing and the sensations in your body.*
- *Create your grounding cord, that tree trunk or waterfall that allows you to release energy and anchor in your body.*
- *Now, consider a relationship that you feel challenged or confused in, or that you would like to take to the next level.*
- *Ask yourself: "What color makes me feel powerful, clear, and good in relationship to this person?" "What color feels best for him or her?" Make sure these colors are different from one another.*
- *Now, imagine two bubbles a few feet out in front of you, one representing yourself and one symbolizing this other person. Make sure there is space between them and ground each one to the center of the earth.*
- *If there is any of your color in the other bubble or any of his/her color in yours, see the colors going back where they belong. As you do this, you are effectively returning each of your energies to your own bodies. You are eliminating confusion over whose stuff is whose, so you can see each other and yourselves clearly. You are restoring attraction and a feeling of spaciousness.*
- *You may complete this one quickly or enjoy the clearing and new awareness as long as you would like before opening your eyes.*

Some women resist this one because they're afraid that separating energies will cause them and their partner to disconnect. From what I have seen, the opposite tends to happen! This exercise causes polarity to return so partners can be magnetized together (in a good way) rather than pushed apart.

I have heard many stories of relationship breakthroughs following this one! This is a good practice to do regularly, even when a relationship is going well, as a form of "energy maintenance."

WHY ARE YOU GIVING?

You might say, "I get why I should love myself and stop fixing my man, yet I can't seem to do it."

This is totally normal. Our spirits and minds are usually way ahead of our emotions and body. We may easily grasp a concept years before we apply it in our lives.

Besides having patience, there is something you can do. Ask yourself: "Why am I giving?" You can apply this to anything, including men. Don't assume it's bad to give, just ask the question.

For example, if you try "fixing" a man out of fear of what will happen if you don't (for example: that you'll be alone, broke, childless, un-loved, embarrassed, etc.), he'll feel that and resist you. If you give to him because you think he's incapable, that can really take him down. Are you doing this because it feels safer, because you feel more in control? If you truly doubt him, it may help to ask why you are with him.

Giving is a wonderful thing, when you give from your overflow, in service to another. There's a fine line between sharing the strengths you have that he doesn't and belittling or overriding him. The difference is the feeling you have inside. The key is learning to distinguish giving from unconditional love from giving out of fear or need.

Next time you feel inclined to give, pause first. Feel and sense in the moment whether you're coming from joy or fear. When it's joy, blaze forward. When it's fear, step back and address the feelings before acting. Try some of the meditations in previous chapters to work through your emotions. Then see if, what, and how you're drawn to share with him.

We are meant to give. The pain of not giving is even worse than the pain of not getting. When we give well, it exponentially elevates the love we share.

PRACTICE: *From Fear and Need to Unconditional Giving*

This is a meditation to heal fearful motivations behind your giving, and to connect to your overflowing heart.

- *Find your meditation space, sit, and ground.*
- *Breathe into your body, and as you exhale, begin to release stress and fear down into the earth.*
- *Reflect on a time you gave to someone because you needed something, or because you were afraid. Or, perhaps you are drawn to give to someone for these reasons now?*
- *Create the image of a big, fluffy rose in full bloom. See it in your minds' eye, a few feet in front of your body, facing you.*
- *Imagine this rose has a "vacuum" action, and that it sucks up all the fear and need that you are ready to release. Any related stories, beliefs, programming, or other people's energy also get drawn into the rose. Take some time with this, and notice what pictures, feelings, or messages arise. Breathe deeply and allow yourself to be surprised. Be curious and innocent as a child.*
- *Once you feel complete with this clearing, notice the rose. Did it change color, get bigger or smaller or heavier?*
- *Next, send the rose off as far as you can imagine, to the edge of the horizon where it goes "poof!" in a burst of light.*
- *Bring your awareness back to your body in this moment.*
- *Create a giant golden sun a few feet above your head. Let this sun attract all your energy back from other people and places, future and past. Call your power back from needing anyone to be or do anything. See rays of gold pouring into your sun, representing your pure life force energy returning.*
- *On your next inhale, allow this golden light to pour through you, especially replenishing the places you just cleared within your body and*

energy field. Replace that fear with trust, love, and your own creative power. Allow the sunlight to radiate completely within your body and aura before you open your eyes.

HOW NOT TO GIVE HIM ENERGY

If you feel like you've lost yourself, if you're not sure what you're passionate about outside of your relationship with him—you might take a look at whether you're giving him energy inappropriately. This is a subtle thing, and it does not necessarily match what you're doing or saying.

For example, I have a client whose ex-boyfriend kept popping into her mind. Even though they were together years ago, even though he's now married to someone else—she knew they were still energetically connected. Her intuition was strong, and she asked me for help.

As it were, she'd been feeling blah lately, lacking in motivation. As much as she meditated and did her self-care practices, she couldn't seem to move forward with her business or dating. Even with the cleanest diet and supplements and expert doctors, her health issues did not resolve. She went to work and through the motions of life as if she were walking through a swamp.

When I took a look, I saw her energy was over with her ex-boyfriend. He wasn't happy in his marriage, but it looked good on paper, so he stayed in it. Meanwhile, his energetic connection with my client kept a spring in his step as it deflated her.

They were in occasional communication, and she knew he'd been doing really well with his business. In the patriarchal model, it's been common for women to give their creative energy away to the men who support them. I think this is why so many women have low thyroid—since the thyroid relates to the throat chakra and creative expression. If it's conscious, it may work for some couples for the woman to play the supporting role. However, I feel this can be done in a way where each person retains their wholeness, and I find more men and women wanting this.

When we give to each other from our overflow, we naturally

support each other without depleting ourselves. This is key—to *give what you have plenty of* and not simply because of his need or yours.

Because my client's former partner was open to the world of energy, I recommended she text him and say, "You've been popping into my mind a lot lately. Let me know if you need to talk. Otherwise, would you please call your energy back."

She liked this idea, and also called her own energy back from him. It would have been easy to blame him for "using" her energy but blame never works. Since she'd been working on boundaries, it was a perfect moment to see where she over-gave in attempt to get love or feel valued and connected.

DON'T RUN YOUR SEXUAL ENERGY THROUGH HIM

This was a shocker when my psychic teacher said it: "Ladies, don't run your sexual energy through a man." Hmmm... I wondered. Isn't it fun to feel the sexual energy flowing with a love interest or new partner? That helps to keep *me* interested. What could be the harm?

My teacher answered it with his next line: "If you do, he'll go for anything that moves." Oh! I realized, if I'm giving him sexual energy when I'm *not* present, he will feel it and want to act on it wherever he is. Of course, there are good conscious men who are faithful, but you don't want to tempt him. Especially if you're not yet dating or in a committed relationship, he has no *need* to choose you, and so you'll want to give him reason to pursue you.

I have firsthand experience with this, and it stings! We women get so mad but in a case like this, the man's not actually "cheating". It feels like that to us because we're invested, we're wired for connection and we feel our energy exchange with him as if it's "real". The truth is that *our* giving to him is fueling what we don't want. The real anger is at ourselves for giving more than we're getting.

You may wonder: what do you do instead? Go ahead and feel the spark when you're with this man. Let your sexual energy flow. Flirt and enjoy your connection. Then, as soon as you're physically apart, see him in his own bubble and come back to your own bubble and body. Feel your sexual energy flowing through your body and let his image dissolve in your mind. Disconnect any energy cords between you and use the gold sun technique to fill yourself back up with any energy you gave to him, consciously or not.

Probably he'll be calling you soon. Meanwhile, the following exercise will help.

PRACTICE: *Calling Your Energy Back from His Life to Yours*

• *Sit in meditation and imagine a man you're interested in, dating, or have been thinking of.*

• *Visualize your tree trunk, waterfall or other grounding cord connecting your hips to the center of the earth. Exhale and relax your body.*

• *Smooth out your aura and choose a color to surround yourself with. See your energetic field radiating 3 to 4 feet out all around you and tuck it in into your grounding cord below your feet.*

• *Consider the man on your mind. With your eyes closed, imagine a bubble or bubbles several feet in front of you, each representing the energy you're giving to various aspects of his life. For example, see a bubble for any relationship he has with another woman. See a one for his work, finances, or home. Ground each of these bubbles, and as you do, drain your energy out of his life.*

• *You are not taking anything that's his here, just releasing what's yours so he can find his own way and experience his own reality. Grounding these bubbles just returns your energy to where it naturally belongs.*

• *As a gesture of support, connect each of his bubbles to the light when you're done grounding them. I like to see a golden stream of light pouring into any person or situation I'd like to help. This affirms the greatest good for that person or situation, without involving me personally. Try it and see it feels.*

• *When you're done, release each of these bubbles fully to the light, seeing them dissolve.*

• *Then fill yourself in with a big gold sun and come out of meditation.*

MEN DO CHANGE FOR WOMEN, JUST NOT WHEN WE TRY TO FIX THEM

It's a fine line between nagging or coaching and requiring something of your man. Again, it's about self-love. When you love yourself, your boundaries naturally fall into place. Yes, please, I'll take cherishing, guidance, and protection. No, thank you, I can't align with flakiness, lies, or abuse. Simple as that. It's not a discussion.

For example, a financially stable women who loves herself rarely chooses a man who doesn't pull his weight (consistently on some level, even if not monetary). By contrast, one who doubts her worth may over-give, and a woman in scarcity might attract a man in scarcity.

The way you live, think, and feel creates an "energy broadcast." If your energy is not aligned with what you say you want in your man, you will tend to coach or nag him. Your need for him to change is a way to bypass your own issues and disown your power.

I'm not saying you shouldn't want a man to change if he doesn't meet your standards. However, there's a huge difference in the way you approach it! By standing in your truth and requiring it of him (sometimes without saying a word), you are more powerful and yet more persuasive. He gets to feel like the man and do it for you. No one, especially the masculine, likes to be nagged into doing things or to feel like they're being reprimanded.

If you choose to speak, an especially powerful approach is to say some version of "I believe in you, I see your greatness, and when you did XYZ, it didn't match who I know you to be." When I did this early in our relationship, my past partner would get quiet, go chant, and wake up a different man the next day. After a couple years, his mother said to me, "You are the best thing that ever happened to him!" She saw so much change.

YOU NOT FIXING HIM GIVES HIM A GIFT

By your standing in your feminine heart, loving yourself, and requiring a conscious man who inspires and honors you, he feels excited and challenged. So far in his life, he likely only changed because he "should." His mother, school, and society all directed him in ways he followed so as not to get in trouble. Probably the "bad boy" inside him squirmed and pushed against this, even if he complied.

The conscious men in his life may have called him out on his stuff. It was probably moderately satisfying to change for his peers or mentors. He did it and felt like a good man because of it.

But then you come along. He feels that rush in his heart that he'll do anything for you. He feels scared that in doing so, he'll lose himself.

And you stay soft and grounded, not settling for anything less than his best self. As he rises to the greatness you see in him, his chest puffs up as if he's just climbed a mountain. He feels on top of the world, like he can do anything.

ASSUME THAT MEN WORSHIP WOMEN

Your light makes his world go around. Why do you think there is a beautiful woman on almost every billboard? He wants little more than to make you shine.

Here, the fact that he was born from a woman works in your favor. The feminine *made* him, in a sense. He is in awe of your creative power. It terrifies him and inspires him like nothing else.

You don't have to be tough like a man for him to take you seriously. Doing business with him? Maybe. But in your love life, that can push him away.

Your feminine energy is already enough. If you quit trying to effort your way and simply drop into it, you will know what I mean.

HOW TO TEACH HIM WITHOUT EMASCULATING HIM

Men take women as teachers all the time, though often not formally. The saying "Behind every great man is a great woman" speaks to this. In a marriage with traditional roles, the wife often holds the vision and provides support for her husband's external success. Without her doing so, he might work the same hours with fewer results.

Now, in modern life, sometimes the man holds space for the woman's vision, and some same-sex couples may take on masculine-feminine roles for combined success. In other cases, the "muse" might be a teacher or daughter or friend—not always a romantic partner.

If you think about it, in order to manifest anything, we need both emotional desire and action. We need both creative expression and structure. In general, the feminine lives life emotionally while the masculine is more achievement oriented. The feminine, at her best, has grace and intuition that inspires the masculine.

So how do you offer your gifts without emasculating him? First of all, however you do it, connect daily to your own body, heart, and soul. When you are steeped in self-care, it will feel natural to care for another. And you'll inspire him to care for you at least as well as you are caring for you.

Another great guideline is "show, don't tell." Correcting or criticizing him won't work. Being a model of grace will. When your heart or intuition don't align with something he says or does, or when you feel you need to direct him in some way, share it with an "I"-statement. For example, say, "I feel so incredibly happy when I imagine us in a new house with three bedrooms and plenty of light," not "You need to buy us a bigger and brighter house you mother-fucker."

"LETTING HIM DO HIS THING"

It had been a year or more since they dated. Every few months, I would hear from her with an "update" after she spoke with him. The story hadn't changed much; he still "wasn't ready" to be in a relationship with her.

Proud of her progress in letting go even a little, my client told me, "I'm doing my best to let him do his thing."

I replied, "It's not yours to let or not let. He's going to do what he does." I could feel the "thump" of truth hitting through her silence.

Her comment revealed her assumption that she got to control what he did. She assumed that even though it had been over a year, even though it wouldn't be healthy even *if* they were dating. If I felt that energy from someone, I wouldn't be "ready" either!

This is one of the ways we women control men unconsciously. Of course, we're hardwired to mother and it's one of the natural aspects of the feminine. However, it belongs with our children, not with our partners. It can be really tempting, however, because men also have their part in it.

MOST MEN HAVE NOT REALLY SEPARATED FROM THEIR MOTHERS

You know the saying, "Girls mature faster than boys?" As I see it, it's not that girls are naturally superior, it's just that we get a running start at birth. All babies are born out of a mother. So, when we girls come out of a female body, we are already in our element. Boys have to separate at some point to become men. At puberty, their voices drop, and they shoot up like beanstalks, generally much taller than their mothers. They love their mothers, but it no longer feels good to be immersed in feminine energy. Their hormones dictate this but attachment between mother and son can make this separation challenging and confusing.

Fast forward to adulthood, and some men naturally have strong feminine sides. Others haven't fully expressed their masculine because they haven't fully "grown up."

Some of these men are totally loving and sweet, which can be attractive to those of us still healing from the effects of patriarchy. However, some men that love to cuddle don't initiate or come through in the bedroom. Some are men who will eat your food for months and never pay for any of it or ever clean up after a meal. These are the men who frequently borrow your car or your money but "aren't ready" for commitments or children.

Author and relationship expert Pat Allen called these men "Peter Pans." They aren't *really* wanting a woman to lead and direct the relationship (play the masculine role) but they aren't taking on that role either. They may even get annoyed when a woman makes decisions for them or judges them as incapable. At the same time, they may not see their own role in disowning their masculine energy.

And what men often don't realize is that most women *really* prefer that men lead. We generally take over either because we're feeling unsafe in our femininity and vulnerability, or because our man is not doing it. We get exasperated and jump in thinking "someone's got to do this."

Usually as women, if we're with a "Peter Pan," some part of us is afraid to let go and receive. And while men have their work to do, our piece is to discover and face our own fears of vulnerability. When we anchor in our self-love and awaken our feminine, it will feel great to be led by a conscious man, and we won't need to fix anyone.

MEN AND BOUNDARIES

Often when men have boundary issues with women, they actually have boundary issues with their mothers. They both attract the partners who will trigger them, and they project these issues onto them.

Men have created all kinds of drama and even ended good relationships, just because they needed to set a boundary with some woman. It could almost be any woman because all they need is someone to stand in for their mother and to claim the boundaries that they never did growing up. This can be healing for the man, and yet painful and confusing for both because it's a response to a past situation rather than to what's happening in the present.

Most of the time this is unconscious. One client said his relationship with his mother was fine now, so he didn't understand why there would be a boundary issue. So, I asked about his childhood and learned he felt totally overpowered by his mother growing up.

Even when something is no longer happening on the surface, it may linger on an energetic level. For example, a man might never speak to his mother but still have a psychic agreement to heal her. This might cause him to feel inappropriately guilty, or worry a lot, or make it hard to access his sexuality.

This is where awareness of *energy* comes in really handy. When you sense these things, you can help your man by expressing your displeasure.

Without analyzing or fixing him, be obviously turned on when you feel his firmness—meaning his solid, masculine energy in every area. Worship him when he is decisive, trustable, and grounded in his body.

When he acts weak and floaty, don't get strong and take over. Don't become his mother, which is what he is unconsciously commanding you to do. Instead, you can get even softer than he is, and see if he comes forward.

PRACTICE: Using a Mirror to Deflect Projection

If you know or suspect that someone is projecting on to you, here is a tool. It's subtle but you'll be surprised at how this makes your life easier.

- *Sit in a comfortable, quiet spot with your feet flat on the floor.*
- *Breathe, close your eyes, and ground yourself.*
- *Imagine a colored bubble a few feet out around you in every direction, marking your sacred space.*
- *Consider someone you feel may be projecting their emotions, desires, or issues onto you.*
- *Now, put the image of a mirror reflecting outward on the outside edge of your aura. This way, when anyone projects on to you, they have to see themselves, and their energy will get sent back to them.*
- *When you're done, fill in with a gold sun and come out of meditation.*

Part 11

YEARNING WITHOUT NEEDING
AND THE ART OF INFINITE CONTAINMENT

Part 11 – Introduction

How do you handle yourself when you really want a man? What if you really do need or desire something from your partner? How and when do you display your yearning without becoming needy? What if, in trying not to be needy, you deny your heart and unknowingly put up a wall?

It's a fine line between yearning and needing. One is a natural feminine quality and one is a distortion. They almost appear the same!

Infinite containment is the byproduct of having both feminine and masculine polarities alive in you. It indicates you're a woman of grace, a woman of wholeness, and it attracts the best from the men around you.

Besides illuminating these distinctions, Part 11 offers additional practical exercises so you can feel into this for yourself. Join me here, and let's take another step into the art of love.

BE YEARNING NOT NEEDY

Desire is your passion pressing beyond yourself into full expression, in collaboration with life. You are here to enliven the world and give your gifts. It satisfies your heart like nothing else to do so.

Need comes from "I'm empty; you have to fill me up." Remember, a masculine man is already empty. He is attracted to your fullness and depolarized by your need.

Your yearning comes from your overflow, from your sensing an ecstatic dance possible and yet unborn. The seed has been planted and as you squint your eyes just so, you see the ground quivering. "When will the beauty burst forth?" you wonder like an eager child. Before your love is actualized, you yearn from the knowing of how good it will feel to give and share.

He wants to give to you, as long as you don't *need* him to do this. He'll proudly take a beautiful, limp flower to the window to give her sunlight, but he won't make that same flower grow out of nothing. You have to get it started. Remember the feminine leads with energy, light, and sweetness.

Knowing that your pain stems from what you're not *giving*, it's easier to let go of need. Releasing the cultural programs of being overly passive and of waiting and depending on a man, you can click into yearning. You can liberate yourself from that ugly state of contraction just by letting yourself feel fully. It's not based on what you "get."

Desire stays and it's not wrong. It's just what's behind it that makes or breaks the outcome.

PRACTICE: *What Do You Yearn For?*

Refer back to Part 3 on the qualities of the true feminine, and to the final exercise in Part 6, where you wrote what you desired to give and receive in a relationship. What are you yearning for now? Paint that picture here, without putting anyone's name on it.

Notes

YOUR NEED REPELS HIM,
OR ATTRACTS HIS CONTROL

When you're needing and expecting that he fulfills you, it's as if you're saying, "I'm nothing, I'm worthless. You make me something." He may temporarily succumb to your demands but in doing so he implicitly agrees with your low self-concept. Over time, this erodes any attraction he had for you and requires you to push harder and harder, or resort to more and more drama. No one feels good here, and it erodes many relationships.

At the beginning, before you "had" him, you wouldn't have dared be so pushy. You knew you had to "put it out" in some way to attract him, and you both enjoyed that dance. Not knowing yet that he "had" you, the possibility of your dating others or not needing him actually drove him to give to you.

As soon as we get close or committed, old programming gets activated. At this point, both men and women tend to become more of what family or culture taught us than is really true for us. Some of this is in our DNA, and it really kicks in when a woman gets pregnant or gives birth. Even becoming exclusive or sharing more intimacy than you're used to can stir things up. So be watchful at these moments. For example, many see marriage as an achievement, when in fact it is a beginning that requires nurturing and continual intention.

Your expressed neediness attracts his reciprocal patriarchal control. He doesn't mean to be the way he's being any more than you mean to be the way you're being. It's just that your operating off of this passive feminine program almost requires it of him. He thinks, "You're gonna whine and pull on me? Well then, I'll show you who's boss!" It comes out of instinct, from what he learned rather than who he is. It comes out of his disappointment that you're not the woman he chose, that you went "crazy" on him. It turns on his self-doubt. He wonders why he didn't see this coming, and out of mistrust in himself and in love, he closes down more. You trigger each other and things spiral down really quickly. The good news is that as long as either one of you change the pattern, you can both get out of it.

In a long-term relationship, of course you are going to need things. See if you can be open about how certain needs get met. For example, money, favors, and conversation—do these always need to come from *him*? Of course, you have your bare-bones requirements for a partner that you created in Part 2. These are personal to you, and if you need your man to have a job or be monogamous, I'm not saying you should stop needing these things. I'm not suggesting you should be so full of money or commitment that it makes up for his irresponsibility. I'm talking about once you meet a suitable man, how to not mess it up.

PRACTICE: *Letting Every Day Be New*

Whether you're in the exploratory phase of dating or in a long-term relationship, this is a great practice. Remembering that exhilaration of getting to know each other, and how "lit up" that you felt, be in that space of "overflow" when you're with him. If your relationship is super established or troubled, or if you've had trauma and cannot remember feeling "lit up," think of anything that brings you great joy—for instance, a sunset, friends or family, or your favorite food. Tap into that feeling when you're with your man (or a man you desire).

Be in a space of appreciation, as if you're on a first date. You're in awe of him and the moment. Get curious about him instead of assuming he's a certain way based on past experience. He'll love you for this; it will feel good to him, even if he doesn't consciously know what you're doing. Not to mention, his old irritating habits might just fade when you quit giving them attention!

Pretending that you've just met, it doesn't occur to you to grasp at anything. You wouldn't dare lean on him because you have no guarantee he'll want a second date. How can you show him the ways you add value to his life?

If you want to attract his generosity, protection, and free-flowing love, you can lean back, breathe into your body, and consciously receive. However, the second you try to control what he's giving you or how he delivers it, you get his control. He is a mirror of you. The reflection you see is both the opposite and the same as what you put out.

WHAT HAPPENS IF YOU DON'T YEARN?

When you live from your fullness, all your feelings have a place. There is an odd feeling of satisfaction even in the midst of tears or anger. You're right there with what's happening. You're free and super energetic because nothing is repressed (and avoiding things really drains your life force!). Since your emotions are moving by definition, you yearn to ride each wave to the other side. You are living naturally.

When you numb yourself to life, you miss the good stuff as well as the bad. Half present, it's difficult to access your yearning. "It's just as well," you tell yourself. "At least I don't have to suffer this way."

One problem here is that he *wants* you to yearn. If you don't yearn, he experiences you as a wall and goes elsewhere. You don't enliven him when you're numb. Besides, his natural masculine wants to give to you, and he cannot give to a wall.

Shutting down is one way to stop yearning. Another way is to fill yourself aimlessly with shallow sex, food, or substances. You may have heard the advice of "circular dating" for women looking to attract a relationship (so she doesn't feel or appear needy). However, this can backfire. It turns off your yearning, which he needs to feel. It can also make you appear unstable or less selective, and therefore less valuable.

The "angry feminist" strategy of not needing anything from a man can also send the wrong message. I think the key here is authenticity. Fill yourself up, take care of your life, and feel your feelings. If in doing so you make money, achieve something, and get happy—your true match will still want you. By contrast, if you become a hardened, driven woman in the name of self-sufficiency— he won't have any opening to enter.

RELAXING INTO YOUR POWER

As a small woman training Aikido with people of all sizes, I have had to find my inner power. I cannot knock a 240-pound man down with my arm alone. However, when I join with his strength and break his balance, I easily throw him using my hips, body, and breath.

The "strength" most of us learned is equivalent to "arm power." Most of us learned that our value lies in what we do, think, and say. The power of our energy and emotions has been grossly unseen and undervalued.

Once you access your inner power, you can relax on the outside. In fact, this dramatically increases your power. Have you ever tried to push over someone who's stiff? It's so easy! If that same person would imagine sinking into the ground, and letting their limbs be loose, you'd have a much harder time.

Remember our manifesting exercises at the beginning of this book? Your emotional power always wins. Having an external concept of what you want is only minimally helpful. This is why I do so much meditation and energy clearing because aligning your energy with your goals is key.

It always takes more energy to be who you're not. If you're perpetually stressed, anxious, and over-reaching with little result, you might want to ask yourself what you've taken on that's not yours. Go into meditation. Use your grounding cord, magic soap bubbles, and vacuum roses to release programming, other people's stuff, and old beliefs.

When do you feel most like yourself? What helps you feel relaxed? Allow yourself these things. It may be scary if you've got the belief that you need to "do" in order to "get." I have seen over and over though how much comes to us so easily when we relax.

THE ART OF INFINITE CONTAINMENT

Even once you relax, heal yourself, and get clear on your desires, sometimes their fulfillment gets delayed. There could be many reasons for this which have *nothing* to do with you. You may be doing everything "perfectly." Now what?

Knowing that feminine energy leads the way, and having a healthy dose of inner masculine, here is your new practice: *the art of infinite containment.* This is a deeper level of not being needy. You are the riverbank to your own river. Your inner masculine "holds" your inner feminine. You emanate love through your body and heart, and therefore you are both complete and pregnant with possibility.

He needs to feel this in you to know you are trustable. If you can "hold" your yearning, anger, joy, pain, all of it—he somehow knows you can hold all of him. To take another step towards you, he needs to know...

Will his energy and life build or dissipate with you? Will he lose himself and drain all his life force? Money? Pride? Trust in love? Are you a safe container for him (sexually and in all ways)?

If you can't contain your own energy, he questions whether he can. He wants your dynamic nature, but he doesn't want craziness that spins his life out of control. Can you simultaneously embody freedom and love, fullness and space? If you can, he's very, very intrigued.

Can you feel the pulsing reverb between your bodies without rushing to act? Are you able to stay soft and neutral, then erupt into a bright smile when he does something sweet? Glare in rage if he's hurtful? Meet him with feisty passion once he gets things started? If you're ready to go any of these places, he feels immeasurably drawn into your stillness.

If he takes his time, don't accuse him of being "chicken" or mock him by believing "girls mature faster than boys." He is trusting you with his heart. I assume you've already screened him to be sure he's a good man. And if so, your judging him here may come more from defensiveness or popular habit than accurate observation. If he's cautious, consider that it may be more about being honorable and choosing well.

Perhaps he's not slow at all, but ready to rush in before you're sure? In this case, you get to lead. Practice your infinite containment and then you will *feel* if he's right for you. You will know the right pace. Either way, appreciate his interest and keep feeling all that you are within.

WHAT HAPPENS IF YOU DON'T CONTAIN IT?

Not containing your energy is the psychic equivalent of gossip, wearing a revealing outfit to a business meeting or giving your valuable skills away for free. It looks like going off in drama, game-playing, hysterics, begging, or attempting to convince him.

These things show that either you don't honor yourself, which is a turn-off (if you don't, why should he?), or you don't have enough awareness or capacity to handle your feelings or his (which makes you less than trustable). So, while it may not *feel* like the most feminine choice to contain all your energy, it's what he needs—at least at the beginning or at times of crisis—to know you can do.

If he does move forward with you, it may be just for a quick fling. He might keep you hanging in a non-committal situation that leaves you confused and wanting. Until you set the precedent that you're the "entire package," why would he see you as such? Men typically get blamed for using women or for being afraid of commitment. To their genetics, sex without love *does* make sense. As frustrating as that can be, it's not a flaw. That said, most men of integrity *will* commit to the right woman who graciously shows him why it's of value to him to do so.

If you have been "holding" all that you are and all that you feel, and he still hesitates, it may be for a very good reason. He may be taking his time to make sure he can measure up. He may be getting his life in order or doing some deep inner work. See if you can remain patient while keeping your options and heart open. That way, you won't inadvertently close the door to something wonderful about to happen.

If you're in an established relationship and your man is in the trenches of conflict or crisis, this is another time to "contain" your energy. Men need to be men and to feel like they're the ones working through problems and making decisions. We get scared of what decisions they'll make, and we want to jump in! Usually that's the last thing they need and can drive them away. It's better to go with "less is more" here—at least on the surface. Truth be told, you are making extremely powerful decisions by how you choose to hold your energy. It goes a long way when he sees that you're safe, drama-free, soft and receptive. At the same time, you can show him you believe he can get through this.

Of course, if *you* need to apologize or change your behavior, or if there's something you really need to say to him—do so. Just think *soft, calm, and clear*. Leave space for him.

YOUR TICKET OUT OF THE HOLDING BACK
OR OVEREXTENDING CIRCUS

It's a fine line, knowing when to freely express your natural feminine heart, and when to contain it. There is a world of difference between holding back due to repression and holding back out of wisdom.

Doing the exercises earlier in this book and feeling all that you feel will eliminate repression as an option. This will give you the internal freedom to choose how and when to express yourself. Not only will you know and love yourself deeply, you'll be able to intuit his level of openness in each moment and act accordingly. From here, you can get creative, and whatever you share is a thoughtful, artful gift.

Overextending is when you do too much, you jump through hoops and bend over backwards to make him happy. You over-give in hopes you'll get what you want. If you ooze sex, if you desperately try to look and smell and act perfect, if you help him or initiate all the time—you're overextending.

Overextending is a symptom of having held back too much or too long, whether you did that with him or just within yourself. It's that pendulum swinging too far towards expression after going too far towards repression. If you've allowed too much of your energy or emotions to build up with no outlet, it can feel really out of control and like you have to do something *now*. For you or for him, it's much more overwhelming to handle years of tears, anger, or desire than it is to deal with today's.

Here's your ticket out of the holding back or overextending circus: (1) feel what you feel—both in yourself and in him; (2) express yourself each day, so things don't build up. Whether you do this alone—perhaps by dancing or journaling or screaming in your pillow—or with him will depend on the feelings you observe. It takes practice. If this is new, start by practicing on your own or with a counselor or friend(s). You'll build this muscle, and before you know it, you'll be able to do this with a partner or a man you're dating.

PRACTICE: *Give Yourself What You Need*

Considering what you're yearning for, ask how you can give those things to yourself now? For example, buy yourself flowers or chocolates if you wish a man would. Give yourself a hug or get a massage. Hire a handyman or take yourself on a romantic vacation. Besides giving to yourself what you wish "he" would, share more of what you would share with him. Deepen your friendships, care more for your family, dance and feel your sensuality. Dress up even on a day at home! Whatever you need to do, get into the feeling of "not waiting" and "having" instead of needing. Remember, yearning comes from overflow, so this won't take away your readiness for love! Write your ideas down here.

Notes

Part 12

COMMUNICATION TIPS

Part 12 – Introduction

We can make or break a relationship with our communication. Communication isn't just words. It also includes energy and body language. While we'll touch on these aspects, in Part 12 we'll look mostly at how we speak to one another.

Words can hurt, soothe, or elevate us. Most of us haven't had the best models of enlightened communication. If you have, wonderful! I've personally noticed an increased collective awareness around conscious, loving, and respectful communication. However, I have not seen much that incorporates feminine and masculine dynamics. And so, this is something I'm going to share here.

Being in your feminine, knowing what the masculine needs and desires, knowing his gifts and challenges and your own—now how do you handle conflict? What's the difference between being artful and playing games? How do you redirect those all-too-human slip-ups?

What if you could make him feel great without over-giving? Are there ways you can speak that will inspire him to step up, without emasculating him? Can your words be a turn-on?

Part 12 will give you tools to do all of this and more. Let's take a look.

CELEBRATE HIM

We women always want more. He gets a big raise and we want more sex. We get more sex and then we bitch about him not helping around the house.

On some level, we keep a list running in the back of our minds of everything that needs fixed. "If only I had X, I would finally be happy." Then we get X and think, "Now I need Y and I'll be secure." We get Y and say, "Now why don't I have Z? This isn't ok!"

It's that feminine creative energy that never stops. We take pleasure in checking things off our list and saying, "What can I create next?" We get excited about it, and he gets crushed. He just wants to win. His masculine eats up the "emptiness" of being "enough."

He wants you to celebrate that big raise, to smile and open your arms with a glow of admiration in your eyes—not to simply check it off and ask him for the next thing on your list. As tough as he may seem, he needs to feel appreciated, and that his efforts are seen and received.

When he shares his victory, this is a powerful moment for you to cheer him on. He is giving you an opening and making himself vulnerable, in a sense. Vulnerability makes us feel more of whatever comes next. Give him applause in this moment and his healthy masculine will grow. Ask him for more and he gets deflated. Years of this can be hard for him to recover from.

LET HIM DRIVE

This is one area where the patriarchy had it down. It doesn't need to be an actual car—or it might be. Letting him lead you in some way is a turn-on, and it's a big part of inviting his masculinity forward.

You might be on the back of his motorcycle; he might be opening the door for you, paying your rent, taking you somewhere brand new, or ravishing you with multiple orgasms. If you trust him and like where he's going, feeling him "take you" anywhere is pretty exhilarating. Your letting him take you makes him want to take you more. It's one of the biggest gifts you can give him.

In conversation, don't let your feminine creativity fill all the quiet spaces. What would be delightful chatter with a girlfriend can blow a man's circuits. With him, let there be silence sometimes. It gives him time to lead the conversation. Be your open-hearted, expressive self, and then artfully pause. This lets you know what he's feeling and thinking about. As much as he enjoys your sharing, he also needs space to relax and feel like a man. Be more responsive, more curious.

Some cringe at the idea of letting him drive, in resistance to traditional gender roles. If you don't want to be taken, ok—just know that resistance is a disempowered stance. It ultimately controls and limits us as much as the thing we're resisting—if not more.

The masculine leading the feminine is a sacred dance. It really has nothing to do with patriarchy when we choose it consciously, free of either old programming or righteous resistance. The more versatile you are with your responsiveness—meaning you have embraced your dynamic nature and loved yourself enough to trust your boundaries—the more empowered you will feel in being led.

Your genuine responsiveness is a gift to him. It goes way beyond him beating his chest because you follow his lead. That's because your authentic response won't always be positive. If he's flakey or hurtful, your raw anger or tears make him a better man. When he knows he can count on your honest feedback in the moment, your love and appreciation mean more. He glows from your compliments and meets you in passion. And when he needs to correct something he does so willingly because he truly cares and because you're not bulldozing him into it.

Remembering the river and riverbank can help. While the river flows where the riverbank goes, the riverbank is constantly being formed by the river. We each lead each other; our ways are just different. Let's enjoy and embrace them.

SHOW HIM YOU TRUST HIM

One of the greatest compliments you can give a man is to let him know you trust him. You can say, "I trust you" out loud, or you can show it through relaxing, opening sexually, or by letting him handle things. This all feels amazing to him when you're in your heart.

There are many facets to trust. There are the big things: you might trust him to not cheat, lie, or steal. Then there are the smaller everyday things, which add up to a lot. Do you trust him to wash his dishes, communicate his thoughts, be on time, and manage his business? These are just a few examples. If, in little ways, you feel you need to manage him, look out. This can erode intimacy and create resentment by whacking his self-worth and exhausting you.

If you don't trust a man, you probably won't want him to lead you anywhere. You might think you do but your hardened body or non-stop thinking tells a different story. Faced with this, he'll instinctively recoil and withhold sex, love, or appreciation. It's a downward spiral where bitterness sets in for each of you.

If you don't trust him in certain ways, please explore this. Is this because he's proven to be untrustworthy, your intuition senses it, or you're working through trust issues? Many times, it's a combination. We will cover intuition in Part 13. As for the other possibilities…

If you *know* he's untrustworthy and it's the big stuff, you may need to move on unless he's seriously changing his ways and you're willing to forgive. If it's the little stuff, you can share your feeling-response (not coaching him) while you practice relaxing, and then see if things shift. If he's a good man who's just not good at certain things, consider how you can set up your day to day lives so you don't have to direct his behavior. For example, with a man who's always late, just tell him 5 pm if you need him there by 5:30. Hire a housekeeper if you need the house clean and he doesn't clean. Get creative and find other acceptable ways to meet your needs while taking the pressure off him and your relationship!

Usually, if you struggle with trust issues—real or imagined—there are deeper reasons. They may come from your past experience, or from something you learned from family or culture. For instance, if your father cheated on your mother, it can make you feel like the other shoe is always about to drop. If your grandmother nagged and micromanaged your grandfather, you might think you *have* to do this. It might feel normal to you or subconsciously necessary for love.

Sometimes, we have traumas we don't remember, either because we were too young or because they were too painful. Even something like having to move houses repeatedly in childhood could make you feel insecure; it doesn't need to be an obvious betrayal. A pattern might have been passed on from one of your ancestors, way before your lifetime, or you may have experienced a breach of trust in a past life. You may be feeling the pain of women you don't even know, since trust has been broken in some ways for all of us.

If you're faced with trust issues, I recommend re-visiting the "Affirmations to Clear Fears and Doubts," Ancestral Clearing, and Forgiveness Prayers in Part 8, and the meditation on "How to Feel Your Emotions and Release Those that Aren't Yours" in Part 6. Consult a professional if the challenges persist, or if you'd like some extra support.

HOW PARTNERS TEST EACH OTHER

Speaking of trust issues, sometimes we deliberately "test" our partners to see if we can trust them. Both men and women do this, and while it's intentional, it's not always conscious.

Once I was close with a man and we felt a strong mutual attraction. He had told me of his fears and his reluctance to get involved. During this time, he did things to test the waters:

- **He told me all about his flaws,** particularly after I expressed interest. (*Will she still like me if she knows this about me?*)

- **He'd disappear without communication.** (*What can I get away with? Will she accept my boundaries? Am I safe?*)

In each case, I knew exactly what he was doing. Hearing his imperfections only made me love him more. It made *me* feel safer, partly because he opened up in telling me and also because it gave me permission to be human. I loved the intimacy in it!

The first time he disappeared, I puzzled over it for days. I asked four friends for their input, one of whom was furious. They all felt it was odd behavior and disrespectful to some degree. I agreed, yet somehow, I felt happy from our connection, and not sad or angry. As soon as I realized he was testing me, I asked him about it.

"That was strange the other night. It seemed out of character how you did that vanishing act. I think of you as really considerate and I didn't feel bad, so I figured you didn't mean to be rude. What happened?"

He gave me a somewhat plausible explanation but what mattered wasn't his words. It was the feeling of heart connection between us that soared in having this conversation. It was the kind of conversation nobody would bother having unless they cared. It showed me I could bring up uncomfortable things with him, that he would receive them graciously.

He got to see that I respected myself but that I wouldn't bash him as I asked for his respect. Because I stayed neutral, he got the safety he was checking for. I could tell by the way he lingered and kept extending the conversation, and I knew he wasn't used to this. Not only did I pass the "test;" the newfound closeness between us was a surprise bonus.

THE SUBTLE DIFFERENCE BETWEEN AN ARTFUL DANCE AND HURTFUL GAME-PLAYING

In the above example, many women would have felt hurt, gotten angry, and sought revenge. Without these types of conscious conversations that my friend and I had, it's easy for the "victim" to become passive-aggressive and for the "perpetrator" to continue distancing or punishing. Nobody wants to participate in these toxic dynamics, yet it takes practice and awareness to not end up there.

We have to take a look at what is really going on, as I did. Seeing everything as a request for love is a good start. Recognizing that there's some misunderstanding behind all blame, we can find our way out. By looking this way, the most difficult moments in our relationships can become our biggest opportunities… our biggest breakthroughs into greater intimacy.

Besides "testing," there is the dance of masculine and feminine we've discussed—where we each start from wholeness and then willingly relinquish roles in order to play in love. When both partners are whole within and awake through the process, the dance is flawless. However, if he avoids important feelings in order to be the rock in her life, or if she clings to him from a place of helplessness—there is a problem. Partners are bound to develop hurt, resentment, or other toxic patterns if they "dance" without checking their foundations first. This is where people really do "play games," such as leading someone on, playing hard to get, manipulating or controlling, purposely making each other jealous, etc. These games don't belong in the dance of conscious love.

HIS ANGER INDICATES INTEREST

Just as it's important not to be afraid of our anger as women, it's also helpful not to *always* shy from his anger. If he's abusive, of course, take care of yourself and get help. If he's a normal human-being that gets mad sometimes, you can work with this energy. Attempting to shut him down shortchanges both of you and the world.

Anger is a natural shade of the masculine drive. It's amazing how when we simply see it for what it is, it feels "clean" all of a sudden. Whether it's about your relationship or his work, you don't have to take it personally. His anger might express his perceived boundary violation or show you what he's driven towards. Try getting interested. Say, "Tell me more about that" and he relaxes, simply sharing passionately what it is for him. Fight or run away and you disconnect, possibly provoking problems and, at least, missing out on feeling his heart.

When he does get angry about you, know he is interested. If he didn't care about you, for instance, he wouldn't get jealous when you talked to that cute guy at work. He wouldn't want you home at night or notice what you wear. You don't have to do everything he wants, of course; just give him space to express it.

His desire and his anger are intertwined. Extinguish one and you extinguish the other. If he succumbs to this temporarily, you may feel like you "won" but over time he'll become bitter and less of who you want. One alternative is to celebrate his anger, and say, "I have a passionate man!" By you getting out of the way and accepting him, he'll likely relax yet retain the best of his fiery qualities. And you both benefit from this.

LET HIM HAVE HIS MOODS

Women are known for being moody, but men have their moods too! One of the most important things I have learned is to stop taking them personally.

Men often need to go off into their "man cave." There are times they don't want to talk, don't want to process, don't even want sex or food. They just need to shut the world off for a little bit. This is where their masculine energy gets re-set.

Sometimes, your man will be angry and punchy. He may go on a rant about work, the government, or traffic. He may go off on you or his friends or family, just because he is tired or needs space. He doesn't always know why he's angry; so contrary to most women's instincts, there may be little sense talking about it. In these moments, you can't fix it. It's no fun to be around—so take a big exhale, leave the room, or let him know if it's really too intense. Remember, there's a fine line between sharing your feelings and coaching him.

I remember one time my man started venting and complaining. He didn't notice but I had headphones on and was listening to affirmations. I pulled one earbud out and said, "What was that? I couldn't hear... I was listening to my affirmations." At this moment, he realized his negativity and stopped. I didn't have to correct a thing! Something like that works really well—just being in your self-care.

If your man gets in a funk sometimes, know that all men have a level of grief innate in their beings. This is because they all have to separate from their mothers in the process of becoming men. Their voices deepen at puberty; they shoot up tall and then go out into the world. As their male hormones take over, there is a bigger sense of loss than girls have in becoming women. Men have to shift out of the female energy they were born in, whereas we rarely have that same shock going from girlhood to womanhood.

The main thing is to remember his mood is rarely due to you. Because of this, you don't need to change anything to fix it. In general, just let it pass. If you can do this and find some humor even, it generally passes much faster.

PRACTICE: Seeing the Truth behind Communication Hiccups

Write about a time you or a loved one felt hurt in your relationship. What was the request for love behind either person's words or actions? What misunderstandings were present? What's the opportunity for a breakthrough into greater intimacy?

USE BODY LANGUAGE

The way you hold your body is powerful. If you walk around tight and tense, you're not open to much of anything—let alone a great man.

Think of how you'd feel after an incredible orgasm—moving through life from your hips with your face lit up, shoulders rolled back, heart and belly soft. If you're already "full" of all this radiance, he cannot resist you. His masculine emptiness is drawn to your glow like a moth to a flame.

This is why movement practices, time out with girlfriends, spa days, or self-pleasuring can be really important for women. Don't wait for him to "give it to you," because your neediness and tightness will repel him! Of course, a conscious man may artfully ravish the tension out of you in these moments (if they're occasional and not the "norm") but most men will recoil. Your stress-filled body not only feels unattractive, but it makes him feel like he's bound to "lose." On the other hand, your openness to him feels like an easy "win."

Some women may be resentful of having to "stoke their own fire," so to speak. This is true in both the old paradigm of passive victimhood as well as in the newer "feminist" tendency to punish the patriarchy for its abusiveness or "failure." Women speaking out, feeling their feelings, and claiming their dignity has been important. To solve the problem though, you must go farther. For now, let go of him and love yourself. This draws a loving man in, and meanwhile you get to enjoy yourself more. It's a guaranteed win for you.

Notes

PRACTICE: *How to Stand, Sit, and Align Your Body to Draw in Love*

If you'd like his masculine energy to come forward, you can physically invite this with your body language. Here are three great ways:

- *Lean back. This is a great one to do on a date. It draws him towards you and shows him you're receptive. Men bond when they invest in you, not when you invest in them. Even though your instinct might be to lean forward to impress him, connect with him, or show your enthusiasm—those instincts can backfire. Enjoy relaxing and notice what happens.*

- *Soften. Soften your heart, your belly, and entire body. Your softness attracts him, allows your energy to flow, and just feels better!*

- *Slow down. Remember you're 140 watts to his 40. As much as he likes you, he cannot match your pace. It's not about limiting yourself, just an exercise to try when you're with him. Play with it. Slow down your breath, your thoughts, your speech, and how much you move. Slowness is sensual. When you do, I bet he'll feel closer to you because here he can fully BE with you instead of just watching you (at best).*

UNDERSTANDING MASCULINE + FEMININE COMMUNICATION STYLES

My man had been preoccupied with work. When he wasn't on a work call or trip and he turned towards me, he talked about work. My days and mind were focused in a different direction, and so it felt like he was talking "at" me, rather than with me.

Twice in the same day, I shared something with him that inspired me. Each time, there was silence for a minute and then he went back to talking about work. I have learned the drawbacks of criticizing a man, so I let it go the first time. But the second time it happened, I shared that it would have felt nice to have some response to my thing before he went back to his thing.

He was surprised. He said if our roles were reversed, and he had told me something about his day and then I went on to talk about my day, it would have been fine with him. Huh? And then I remembered something one of my psychic teachers taught me about male and female communication styles.

I can see her now. "Here's how two men communicate," she said as she held up one palm. The first man says, 'How 'bout them Braves?'"

Then she put out the other palm (for Man #2). "Work's been really busy lately."

It was an exaggeration, but we giggled and got the point. The masculine thinks about one thought at a time. There's a compartment for everything. The feminine, by contrast, sees everything as interconnected. We naturally find ways to relate with the person we're speaking with, and it feels rude if that doesn't happen.

Here's one example of a feminine-type conversation:

"My daughter didn't sleep well last night."

"Oh, I'm sorry. I don't have kids, but I have a cat who jumps on me in the night. I can imagine how that must affect your sleep."

"Yeah. I had a cat once…"

Most of us women will go out of our ways to find connection. By nature, men don't see or look for connections.

It doesn't mean they don't care. It's just that their brains work differently. They are actually shocked sometimes when our feelings get hurt. This is why God gave us girlfriends! And meanwhile, we can try not to take it personal when the men around us are just being themselves.

ADDRESSING CONFLICT IN ONGOING RELATIONSHIPS

In ongoing relationships, sometimes we women don't address the issues that need attention. Instead, we wait and hope for the man to change or initiate a dialogue. Sometimes years go by and we're talking to girlfriends, a therapist—everyone but our partners! While it's healthy to let some things go, and to process some things without involving him, it's important to communicate about the big things. The question is, how can we do this effectively?

It's true that saying, "Stop doing XYZ" or "I want you to ABC" will likely seem too masculine. This directness works on occasion, but he generally responds better when we state the facts and then own our feelings about the facts. For example, "When you drink a six-pack every night, it feels like you aren't 'here.' I feel sad and lonely. I'm scared to see our daughter growing up with this.' This kind of statement gives him the opportunity as a man to "fix" your problem, instead of telling him *he* has a problem. He may admit his shortcomings if you lead from your own vulnerability. Here, you inspire his empathy and courage and he'll feel much closer to you.

By contrast, making him wrong puts him on the defensive from the get-go, and makes it unlikely that you'll get what you want. If you're too upset to take the suggested approach, I recommend taking some space to process your emotions before speaking to him. Just don't wait too long or your conversation will seem out of context and possibly "crazy."

Here's another example that enlists his support in a challenging situation: "When you say you'll do X and then you do Y, I feel like I can't trust you. When I can't trust you, it's hard to open up, like I'm on guard all the time. You say it's a turnoff when I'm stressed out, so can you help me relax? Here's something you could do..."

Giving him a specific request gives him hope. While he might feel overwhelmed, confused or incapable in solving your big issue—he knows he can do one thing. If him giving you a massage, being on time for a kid's birthday party or going out with you on Friday night would make you feel better— let him know. He loves short and sweet—bullet points coupled with feelings. Try this and I believe you'll both see progress.

It's especially powerful to share our body sensations, either through our expression and movement, or by naming them out loud. For example, offer a bright smile, a big hug and kiss, or literally jump up and down when you're happy with your partner. Express things like "When you talk about your ex, I feel squirmy in my stomach like I want to throw up."

He may be able to argue with your thoughts, but he can't argue with your feelings and bodily sensations. He'll get your message, and because he wants to feel your bodily-expressed pleasure, he'll want to change—without you telling him to do it.

PRACTICE: *The Sandwich Method*

When you need to criticize a man or ask him to change, you can use the sandwich method. Surround the "meat" or criticism with two positive statements, and he'll be able to hear you.
It looks like this:

1. *"I know how much you love our family and how hard you work to provide for us. I adore our house and I'm so glad I don't have to worry about the bills."*
2. *"When you travel for work and I'm alone with the kids for days on end, it's really overwhelming. I'm going nonstop from 6 am to 10 pm. I'm not getting enough sleep or exercise or self-care and I'm eating whatever I can grab. I feel like I'm losing myself and I know that's not what you want."*
3. *"Would it be possible to keep your trips to four to five days, or what are your ideas to solve this? I really want to have energy to give to you too."*

With #1, you validate him (authentically) so he can hear the rest. In #2, you let him know the problem (without blame). Then #3 is your request for improvement and your vision for what's possible.
Try the sandwich method and see how it works for you!

BEING IN INNOCENCE

After doing thousands of readings over two decades, mostly on relationship questions for women, one thing is clear. Most women try really, really hard at this stuff! I was telling a male friend of mine how two-thirds of the questions I get were women asking, "Why did he disappear?" or "Will we be together?" And his eyebrows went up, like he was thinking, "Wow!"

As women we are wired for love. I've done it too, obsessing over these types of questions because nothing matters more to me. But, of course, when love is flowing, we aren't trying or obsessing. It just happens.

You can probably think back to one of those giddy moments where you're flirting, connecting with a love interest, or on a great date. In that moment, you're not thinking at all—you're simply in it. The conversation just flows, the sparks fly, the hands move right where they need to go. There is nothing you can do to stop it. This is what we all yearn for. Yet we forget.

Be innocent, be silly, be tender. Let your heart overflow with your giving. You don't have to *try* to be feminine or do something to bring out his masculine. These are facts of nature. I've written this book to help you un-learn and remember some things but, really, you know.

Part 13

TRUSTING YOUR INTUITION
IN RELATIONSHIP

Part 13 – Introduction

Since thousands of clients have asked for my intuitive insight on relationships, I thought I'd offer some tips so you can do this for yourself! If you're like me, you've probably been psychically connected to your love interests and partners for years—so, really, it's not about learning how to do it. More so, it's about understanding what you're picking up and using your abilities in a way that supports your success in love.

From choosing the right partner or knowing whether your crush likes you back, to navigating the confusing moments of dating, to maintaining balance and attraction in your marriage—this section covers it. Even with powerful emotions or hormones rushing through you, imagine having the tools to drop in and find your answers.

Beyond the everyday, Part 13 explores what it means to have a "soul connection" with someone, and how to create a partnership based in shared purpose. You'll also receive meditations to clear up karma and intuitively "read" any relationship.

Have fun with these!

HOW TO TELL IF HE'S INTERESTED

At times I had dreams about a guy I liked, and I felt his energy around me. I'd be lying on the couch at 11 pm reading a book when suddenly I'd feel turned on as his image would flash in my mind. I couldn't help but wonder what he was doing in that moment!

These "out of the blue" experiences are clear indicators that you're picking something up. When you see a specific person's face and you weren't already thinking of them, there is a reason for that. It's easy to feel like you're making things up but it's harder to make it up than it is to sense accurately.

Especially when your body responds, that's a double indicator that something is up! Just as you feel a certain way after eating something delicious, being physically touched, or receiving a compliment, your body responds to psychic energy.

We covered clearing energy cords back in Part 6. Just as during physical lovemaking, it is natural for someone to send a cord your way as they fantasize about you. This can go into your heart, sexual centers, or other spots, depending on the nature of their thoughts.

It's not always racy. Immediately upon sending a warm text to a love interest, I remember smiling uncontrollably and feeling a huge rush in my heart. It was noticeably different than the nervous feeling I'd had before sending my message. So, I knew instantly how he felt upon reading it.

PRACTICE: *Sensing How He Feels about You*

To test someone's feelings for you, you can daydream about them and see how your body and heart respond. Does it feel like that channel is open or closed? Is there mutual excitement or are you forcing things?

Before texting or calling or speaking, you can imagine what you'll say and imagine his response. It's not really imagining but it feels like that to begin with. If you feel yourself hitting a brick wall, if your body stays closed, or if your heart feels blah, he's either not interested or it's not a good time. Try this with different people at different times, in different situations. Having a variety of experiences will help you discern and interpret things more and more clearly.

Be sure to release any energy cords you created, consciously or not, after doing the above exercises. To do this, just picture any cords vanishing and each person filling in with their own light.

Then call your energy back to yourself with a gold sun. Sensing how he feels isn't the whole answer, as we'll cover soon, but it's a good step.

SEEING HIS GREATNESS WITHOUT LIVING IN FANTASY

A lot of women live in fantasy when it comes to men and relationships. If this is you, you see what he's capable of, and even though he's not acting that way, you hold on hoping. This is a version of the "toxic responsibility" we covered in Part 10. It can waste years or months of your time and can prevent your being outrageously happy with a great guy.

You could be the most inspiring woman in the world and still some men would not change. They aren't ready to. He might love you deeply, just not be able to act on it due to life circumstances. He might still be attached to self-doubt, addictions, abusive patterns, or financial struggle. Probably, it has nothing to do with you.

Of course, there are times when a guy who "wasn't ready" does "man up" after meeting you. It takes discernment to recognize when this is the case. If he's committed to personal evolution, he'll show signs that he is. You'll feel his heart wanting to and you'll see him move in that direction. Watch for signs and ask your friends and trusted advisors if they see these as real indicators or fantasy-hopes.

Women are feeling-oriented, and so sometimes it helps us to check the facts and put things in perspective. For example, if you tolerate his meanness because of your sexual chemistry, dependence, or lack of self-worth, I'll bet your friends see it clearly. Ask yourself, "Would I let a friend treat me the way he's treating me?" On the other hand, you might be writing him off and your friends or advisors see hope. Get support.

Everything you've done up until now to manifest your ideal love, heal your past wounds, and clear your energetic field comes into play here. All this has prepared you to distinguish your intuition from hope, fear, and doubt.

Pick a moment when you feel clear and relaxed, perhaps after meditation or yoga or a good night's sleep. Then ask yourself, "Do I *feel* my relationship shifting in a good direction?" "Does my body say 'stay'?" "Do you see him evolving as time goes on?" "Does he meet the criteria for a conscious man?" (You'll discover the criteria in the next exercise.)

Check in with your personal requirements. He may be a "good man" but if you require commitment, a certain lifestyle, or something else that's just not happening—get out. Sometimes your boundary will inspire him to change but it's important to do this simply because you're worth it.

What if he's married or has a girlfriend? This is a common one. If it's your situation, it's possible you have a true knowing that he's meant for you. Tread carefully. Even if that's true, you don't want the karma of interfering; you'll want to let him make that choice.

More often, women choose unavailable partners because they themselves aren't available. Choosing a man who's emotionally or physically distant is another version of this. There's nothing wrong with taking some space for yourself, and in some cases being (mostly) alone is a healthy choice that gives you the best of both worlds. For example, having a long-distance partner or emotional affair gives you lots of personal space while still having some love in your life. The pain comes in when you pine away for more. If you're doing so, you may be ready to heal whatever in you has made you unavailable. It may be time to revisit the exercises earlier in this book so you can clear up past hurts and unhelpful stories.

Besides sensing his willingness to grow, this brings me to the other important factor: YOU. Are you doing your part? Are you complimenting his greatness, showing your trust where applicable, embracing your natural feminine, and healing and expressing yourself? Are you giving your heart's gifts?

By the time my daughter's father and I got together, I had learned to do the above. Our relationship didn't "make sense," yet I'd heard a voice from the very start that said, "This is the man you're supposed to be with." We were both just out of breakups, I moved back to LA where he didn't want to go, he followed me then broke up with me four times. Even with all this, I stayed in my heart, took care of myself and encouraged him without over-giving.

Those first few months challenged me a great deal, but they didn't break any of my requirements. In fact, it stretched me in a good way to trust more, enjoy more, and stay strong in myself.

PRACTICE: *How to Pick a Conscious Man*

Picking a conscious man is important because otherwise you can do everything right and it still wouldn't work! When it comes to a man whom you're with or are considering as a partner, fill this out for a good starting point:

☐ *He has a practice, a mentor, and/or community to keep him accountable and on course (on his personal path of greatness). He uses these resources regularly, and when he gets triggered.*

☐ *He shares his thoughts and desires with clarity and openness.*

☐ *While he may sometimes be private, he seems comfortable with his emotions.*

☐ *More often than not, he demonstrates sensitivity to your needs, energy, and feelings.*

☐ *He has moral principles that he lives by.*

☐ *You trust him.*

☐ *He is considerate of his family, friends, and the world around him.*

☐ *When you express your emotions in the moment, he remains calm and doesn't react inappropriately.*

☐ *He shows respect and avoids blame when speaking about previous partners and life experiences, even when things were challenging.*

☐ *BONUS: He shares the lessons and gifts he received from past challenges, perhaps even with a sense of humor.*

If you don't have at least seven out of ten boxes checked, this man will likely disappoint you—no matter what you do. It doesn't mean he's a bad guy and it's not your job to teach him. You are learning the difference between an evolving soul who grows through your light, and a less-awake man who just cannot meet you at this time.

Ultimately, picking a conscious man is an exercise in self-love!

WHAT IS YOUR PURPOSE?

Purpose is more of a masculine concern; however, you'll be much more likely to have a healthy relationship with the right man if you know yours. For example, knowing you prefer to be a mother and homemaker, you'll more easily find a man who supports you in doing so. By contrast, your draw to run an international foundation requiring constant travel would pull in a different sort of man. As a writer and intuitive, I've realized I need a man who lovingly allows me the time and space I need for reflection.

It's not necessarily more feminine to stay at home raising kids. In today's world, we are re-defining masculine and feminine. Societal roles don't define us; energy does. You could be in your full creative expression, flowing and feeling and responding to life while also making tons of money or leading an organization. A man could "hold down the fort" and be the "rock" in the family, as long as he feels purpose in that. His drive might go into a hobby or project that doesn't make money but completely fulfills his masculine and serves the world.

In the case of one couple I know, she is more visible in the world. Yet he travels with her, like an anchor that allows her to shine brighter. The way he looks at her and speaks of her, it's as if he's the King worshipping the Queen.

Besides getting the right man, you'll want to know your purpose in order to have a relationship based in wholeness rather than co-dependence. There is nothing wrong with supporting his purpose, if you realize that's yours to do. But if you're just saying, "Yes Dear" all the time without knowing who you are, that's a problem.

If you're already in a relationship, it's never too late to consider your purpose. From time to time, re-visit this question because purposes can evolve. Bring your realizations to your partner and ask him to share his purpose. Then, look at how you can support one another.

KNOWING THE PURPOSE OF YOUR RELATIONSHIP

Knowing your purpose and finding a man of purpose are great steps. For your relationship to last and remain fulfilling, you'll also need a shared purpose. My teacher used to say that the couples he saw breaking up had "stopped creating together."

Some couples raise children, and some collaborate in work. Others take joy in shared community activities, hobbies, their home, or travel. You don't have to do everything together but it's important to do some things together.

"Shared purpose" can also run deeper. Maybe you're here to ground him and he's here to expand you. You may be completing past life karma, or—because of how well you two complement each other—you might bring out the best in each other, causing you to undo old patterns.

It's rare for a couple to come together with no purpose. Still, it's worth exploring what your shared purpose is to make sure it's productive for the long term. Your shared purpose can change over time. If you've been together for a while, I recommend re-visiting this question periodically, and together re-committing to a purpose you both stand behind. If you're single, it's a great time to consider what purpose you would like your next relationship to have!

PRACTICE: *Exploring Your Purpose in Relationship*

Take out your pen and answer the following questions. Don't worry about getting it perfect; just start where you are today! Just by asking these questions, your answers will come, and your life will unfold in more meaningful ways over time.

What is my individual life's purpose?

What is the purpose of my relationship?

Explore this one with your partner if you have one. If you're currently single, what purpose would you like your next relationship to have?

HOW TO KNOW IF HE'S "THE ONE"

First of all, I don't believe there's only "one" person for each of us. I feel we have many potential soulmates from which to choose. I believe that each soulmate has a different purpose, and not all of them are meant to be life partners. Some are meant to wake us up and teach us lessons or set us on a path. Others may be partners or friends for a period of time, and some are lovers for a lifetime. To find the right one for you, it's important to get honest about what you want. Frequently, your higher self knows that better than you do. This is why life is always giving us what we need, even when that's not what we want or think we are getting!

That said, there are certain "standout" relationships that come along rarely. Think back to past partners or guys you've been interested in. Some you may barely remember! You may wonder how you ended up together, considering how little you had in common. Others changed your life. You'll never forget them because you sense the huge purpose you shared together, or the significant impact you made for each other. Whether you met once or created a family for a lifetime is less important in these cases.

Earlier in this book, you learned exercises to attract the relationship you desire. It's completely valid to want a marriage or children or other "externals." I've also offered practices to help you trust your intuition to determine your right partner.

Next, I'll share an exercise to guide you in attracting a soul-level love. This can absolutely co-exist with the rest of the "package" you choose.

PRACTICE: *Meditation to Connect with a Soulmate*

- *Sit in a comfortable spot with your feet on the floor and eyes closed.*
- *Let your body soften on each exhale and imagine drawing your own light to you with each inhale.*
- *Create your grounding cord—a tree trunk or waterfall flowing down from your hips and deep into the center of the earth.*
- *Breathe into your heart. Feel into the love you have within you, to give. What color is it? See if you can allow more breath in as you let the warmth of this love grow within you.*
- *Notice your crown chakra, like a blooming lotus flower at the top of your head. Remember the Universal love you connected with in Part 1—that infinite stream of golden light filling you from above? Re-affirm this connection now.*
- *Now, from your crown chakra, from your soul to his, send a "hello" out to your soulmate. You don't have to know "who" it is or "how" you will meet. Just know that as you circulate the love within you, you are a magnet for your soul "match." That special person who can meet you on every level will be attracted to you when you're here.*
- *As you send out this "hello," notice if any specific pictures, feelings, or messages come to you about your soulmate. You might hear an inner voice or have a thought pop into your head. You may get a sense of what he looks like, where you will meet, or what you need to do to get ready. If the impressions you receive are more subtle, don't worry. Some people simply sense a warmth or a flash of color. In these cases, have a childlike sense of wonder and ask what the information means. Enjoy this as long as you would like.*
- *When you feel complete, thank him and let him know you're going back to your day for now. Let him know you'd love to meet again and invite him to find you in 3-D life when you're both ready.*

- *Fill yourself from head to toe with a golden sun and come out of meditation.*

Note: Sometimes this sense of someone "in your field" will happen spontaneously. You may dream of him or just feel his presence in your quiet moments. Once, I couldn't stop listening to a song titled "Is There Anyone Out There?" in the months before meeting a soulmate. I had no idea until later why I kept playing that song!

With my daughter's father, I had actively been calling in a partner to have a child with, and then the specific guidance I received about him happened right before going to sleep one night. I saw that I would meet my man at a raw foods retreat in Arizona. Later, an intuitive friend saw him in my field, and commented that him coming into my life would be like getting a spaceship to land. I DID meet him at a raw foods retreat in Arizona months later, though it took us another year to start dating. And he is very "cosmic." I still laugh when I remember the spaceship comment!

HAVE YOU HAD PAST LIVES TOGETHER?

The most intense relationships are often with those souls we've known before. These can be incredibly fulfilling because the level of love that's been cultivated over multiple incarnations can be profound.

On the other hand, some of the most toxic relationships also fall in this category. Recently, a client called me back months after our last reading. She told me, "You said my boyfriend was cheating on me and lying about it, and you were right." Then she proceeded to ask for details about his relationship with the other woman, how long they would date, and whether he'd cheat on her too. At some point my screen went blank.

"I'm not being shown that," I told her. "Besides, no matter what answer I give here, it wouldn't make you happy. I'd love to look at how to support *you*. What I'm really wondering is why you're wanting a guy who cheated and lied."

She went back to ask me her initial questions. I reiterated my commitment to support *her*, and that in keeping with my integrity, I couldn't look anymore at him and the other woman.

I said, "You might want to call someone else on that one." I was ready for her to hang up, but she didn't.

I said, "Clearly you're struggling with this, so I'm looking at how you can stop struggling." I then saw a painful past life she'd had with this man, and I helped bring forgiveness to the "unfinished business."

This is a common example of the magnetic pull these karmic connections can have. They range from off-the-charts love affairs to toxic pits to avoid at all costs. For this reason, I recommend the following meditation.

PRACTICE: Getting Free of Difficult Karma

• *Sit in meditation, close your eyes, and notice your inhalations and exhalations.*

• *Ground yourself to the center of the earth and pat your body to increase your presence here and now. Perhaps notice any sensations of pleasure and let this expand as you notice them.*

• *Consider one intense or difficult relationship you have or have had.*

• *Next, in your mind's eye, imagine a ring a few feet out in front of you. Instead of a full circle, imagine it has a gap in it. The size of the gap will show you the amount of karma, or unfinished business, you have with this person.*

• *To complete the karma, spin the ring in your mind until you see a full circle. Then, toss it off to the Universe with thanks.*

• *You may need to repeat this more than once with a difficult relationship. Keep seeing your circle complete with a sense of peace, freedom, and letting go. You'll start to notice a change.*

CULTIVATING YOUR PSYCHIC CONNECTION WITH HIM

He lived about 5 minutes from me, and so I often drove by his house, because it was on my way. I remember one night seeing his car on my way home, then standing in my kitchen talking to him out loud. I said, "This is Ann…" (psychic courtesy) and then proceeded to tell him how stupid I thought it was that we were both home—only 5 minutes apart—when we could be together. I said I knew there was a great connection between us. I spoke until I was exhausted.

When I shared this with a friend, she said, "He *is* stupid." Still, I felt incomplete, and I didn't speak up when I saw him in the flesh. What I didn't feel, though, was stuck. I longed for him, yet my ability to voice my emotions (even in a room by myself) gave me a sense of freedom that I want for my clients today. When you can't stop thinking about a man and can't reconcile your feelings with what's "actually happening," having a telepathic conversation like this is so useful!

Years later, that man and I spoke about our connection and what was going on at that time. I know now that I was "heard," even though it was not evident in the moment.

In some cases, having a telepathic conversation and especially moving your emotions will bring an immediate shift! For example, a past lover had stopped communicating with me and I felt unresolved. At home by myself one day, I said a prayer for healing, then yelled at him out loud and told him everything I needed to say. The next day I saw his truck ahead of me on a highway neither of us normally took. I pulled up next to him and motioned for him to pull over. Because I had "gotten it all out," I didn't need to yell in his face, and our meeting gave me the resolution I needed.

Another time, a love interest introduced me to someone in a way that diminished our relationship. It wasn't appropriate to speak up in the moment, but I telepathically let him have it that night. I told him it hurt my feelings and made me mad because he wasn't owning the truth. His words and actions weren't unified, and I called him out, knowing he valued integrity.

The next day, he introduced me to someone in a different way—a way that was much more "true." It felt so much better!

The day after that, he introduced me to yet another friend. This time, he said the complete opposite of what he said on Day 1. I hopefully played it cool but inside my jaw dropped! It was downright exciting how much he valued me by his comment. And I hadn't said a word out loud to him about this.

In any kind of ongoing or close relationship, you have an energetic connection. That means you can speak to the other person telepathically before or instead of having a verbal conversation. This is useful when you're not sure he'll hear you, or when you want to stay in the feminine role. To do this, you can speak to him out loud when he's not around, speak to him in your mind, or write a letter that you don't share. Or, from your meditation, send him the picture from your heart. Because you're already connected, he will receive these messages on some level.

From romance to business to parent-child relationships, we generally make our energetic connections and agreements before we meet physically. Many times, when reading a client, I've noticed a partner in her field who hasn't shown up yet in the flesh. This is how we psychics can see a strong probability that someone is coming for you.

So, whether you're struggling in a current relationship or looking to call a partner in, you can use your intuition actively to cultivate communication. This is another level of using your feminine creative energy in balance with your receptive energy.

MOMENT BY MOMENT INSTINCTS: HOW TO KNOW WHAT TO SAY AND DO

Besides attracting a soulmate and navigating relationship stress, there are so many small decisions we make every day in our love lives. *Should I text him or not? What should I wear? What should I say? How do I handle my fears about his ex? Can I ask him out or do I wait for him? Should I offer to pay on a date? How soon should I sleep with him?* These are just a few of the questions I hear frequently from clients.

The more you hone your intuition, the more it will guide you in all these things, moment-by-moment. Here are some of the ways you'll get your answers:

- **You'll hear a voice in your head,** like a loud thought that comes "out of the blue." For example, I'll hear "say it," "not now," "don't say it" or "wait" when I'm wondering whether to say something.

- **Your body will move in a certain direction**. You may just start doing something with gusto, even when you don't know why. Or, if you can't bring yourself to kiss him, pick up the phone, or pull out your wallet to pay for something—that may also be your body's wisdom guiding you.

- **It will feel right or wrong.** That red dress that looked great a few days ago now feels completely wrong for the party—because your mood and energy has shifted. Trust that.

- **Something helpful will cross your path in an unusual way**. This could be a piece of information, a "sign," or a significant person showing up.

- **You'll "imagine" his response and you like it (or don't).** As we just covered in the section on "Cultivating Your Psychic Connection with Him," your "imagination" is one of your intuitive superpowers. Play with it by picturing different ways of saying or doing something until you like the response you feel from him.

As you do all of the above, you'll want to be authentic. This may sound obvious but it's *so* important. Being *too* good at tuning into others (especially men) is quite common for women, and we're often asleep to this skill that we have! If you have it, it can cost you in many ways:

- "Losing yourself" in relationships
- Getting into dysfunctional relationship patterns that don't honor you
- Over-focus on being "perfect"
- Not allowing him space because you're always energetically tracking him
- Attracting the wrong partner or an inauthentic partner (because we receive what we put out)

I know how scary it can be to show him your less-perfect side. The feminine can be messy and we weren't taught to show those parts of ourselves. The baby-maker inside us wants everything perfect. Our programming says "a good girl" is X, Y and Z. We're scared he'll reject us if he sees our fears or ego stuff or "crazy" side.

I believe he finds it fascinating. Our personal quirks are what make us lovable. Being open about your "weird" or "dark" side shows him that: (1) you're confident, and (2) you trust him. Remember, both of those things are major attraction-boosters! Pulling your energy out of him, so that you're full of your own radiance, is also a big plus.

Your being vulnerable gives him reassurance that he can be vulnerable too. I believe it lets him off the hook (in a good way) when you take responsibility for yourself, rather than over-focusing on him.

From an "energy" perspective, your authenticity means that

you're in your body. One major pitfall with trying to be perfect is that it's unnatural and uncomfortable. In this state, our bodies get tight and we tend to disconnect from them. Of course, if you're out of touch with yourself, you can't connect to anyone else. He would rather feel your rage or nervousness over feeling "nothing." His masculine is already "empty"; he chose you because you give him "something." You'd be surprised at how many things he'd prefer over nothingness. In addition, when you're "not home" in your body, you tend to pick up more energy from your environment. This causes a lot of confusion for you both and creates a downward spiral by making it harder to reconnect to yourself.

IS IT FEAR OR INTUITION?

This is one of the major issues that comes up when I teach intuitive development. How can you tell if that voice in your head is just your fear or a real message? Are you picturing something because you want it or because it's really happening?

Welcome to interesting territory. I will answer these questions, and meanwhile, they bring me to mention another one of your powers:

You are just as good at projecting as you are at receiving.

If you picture something you desire, it *does* help you get it. Feeding those fears in your head *will* make them more likely to play out. This is where we get into quantum physics, where the observer always influences whatever s/he's observing. There is nothing completely objective; no situation is outside your influence. This is where all the self-healing work we've talked about comes in so you can become a conscious creator, using emotions to your advantage rather than being at the mercy of them. Doing your meditation and clearing karma, past wounds, and others' energy is a huge help.

Even after decades on a path of personal growth, you'll get stuck and confused at times. So, here are some keys to distinguishing fear or hope from true intuition:

- **Your intuition whispers**. It doesn't shout. It doesn't spam you and it's not like a record stuck in a groove. It feels like a wise friend, even when it reveals something you'd prefer not to see.

- **Intuition pops into your mind**, with a feeling of "where did that come from?" You may have a sudden "a-ha," a thought that doesn't feel like you, or an illuminating dream. Frequently, when asked about a person (living or dead) in a reading, I will get a message from them to give to my client. In my mind, I'll hear that person speaking in a way I would not normally speak. So many times, I've relayed the message just as it was given and been told, "That sounds just like him!" In contrast to these distinct intuitive impressions, your fears seem familiar and come with a feeling of "Here we go again!" If something painful happened in your past or to one of your loved ones, you are more likely to fear it. So, meditate to release what's already happened, reclaim your power from it, and *then* ask for guidance on the current situation.

- **Check the facts**. Despite what I said above about nothing being objective, if you're afraid he's out with another woman, it can bring great comfort to get on Facetime and see him alone at home. I'm not advocating snooping, but I do recommend facing a situation. Here's where you may need to get vulnerable and say, "I'm afraid of such and such," or "I had this picture pop into my head. Is it true?" Of course, people can lie to you but your leading with honesty paves the way for a better outcome. And it's a good practice to sense whether the response you get feels true.

- **Observe body language**. If someone fidgets or regularly won't make eye contact, that's a red flag. If *you* feel sick to your stomach or you wake up like a kid on Christmas Day, those are indicators that you're picking up on something. Sure, your stomach can churn when past pain gets re-stimulated, so be sure to follow the guidance above for self-healing and getting to know your triggers.

SPOTTING RED FLAGS

My friend next door was sitting on her porch looking serious. "What's up?" I asked as I walked up her steps.

"I'm seriously considering ending my relationship," she told me. She went on to recount all the ways her man wasn't meeting her needs. I held space and just listened.

Her relationship was unlike any she had known before. As our conversation unfolded, she realized all the gifts she was getting from him. So many of her "unmet needs" revealed themselves to be outdated expectations based on old patterns. Her freak out wasn't really about her partner's actions as much as it was about her changing her pattern. Because she was going into unknown territory, she didn't feel safe.

What she thought were red flags weren't. I think my being there, even silently, helped her to see the truth. I see this a lot, and Gay Hendricks refers to this as an "upper limits" problem in his book, *The Big Leap*. When life gets better than it's ever been, we often put the brakes on to get back to comfort. I've had many clients come to me with "red flags" that were actually big breakthroughs.

Equally common are the women who tolerate lies, disrespect, and abuse because those things feel familiar. I am shocked at what they accept, but somehow, they keep talking themselves into staying in their situations.

Because we're all creatures of habit, this is where asking friends or trained professionals can keep you on track. Having a spiritual practice to re-center yourself daily is so important.

And remember, as we discussed in Part 1, true love is not concerned with your comfort. It will annihilate your ego by wiping out everything that is not love. The more you choose love, watch out; you will likely be challenged.

There's a difference between being challenged and being

punished. Abuse is challenging in the punishing sense. Breaking up with a lover that wasn't your true match may hurt but it ultimately gives you more than it takes.

Ask yourself anytime you're looking at a possible red flag: *Am I being stretched beyond my comfort zone, or is this situation actually harmful?*

When you don't know, ask for support. Friends, healers, or counselors will be able to see into your blind spots.

PRACTICE: *Using Your Intuition to "Read" a Relationship*

This is a great way to get a general "read" on any relationship!

• *Sit in a comfortable spot with your feet on the floor and close your eyes.*

• *Create your grounding cord, sending it down into the center of the earth and exhale.*

• *Think of the two people you'd like to "read" in relationship to each other. This could be you and another person, or two people besides yourself.*

• *A few feet out in front of you, on the left side, picture a rose representing Person A. On the right side, picture a rose representing Person B. Leave some space in-between. Because these aren't "real" roses, they could be any color or even some other symbol entirely. Trust the imagery you see.*

• *Notice the colors, quality, shape, and size of each rose. Now, make up a story about them. For example, let's say your rose is fluffy pink, facing his dark green rose with thorns facing away from yours. I might interpret this to mean you're feeling bubbly and loving, while he's protective and distant, maybe going through a deep growth process. If you saw two roses each facing upwards, this might mean each person is more focused on their own path or purpose than on the other.*

• *Once you have a sense of where each person is at relative to the other, envision a rose in-between Rose A and Rose B. This one represents the relationship.*

• *Just as you did with each individual's rose, study the relationship rose and then say, "What is this image telling me?" If it's a bud, perhaps it's a new relationship or an old relationship with a new beginning. By contrast, petals falling off could indicate a completion of some sort.*

• *With all of these roses, bright and clear colors indicate health and vibrancy; whereas muddy colors indicate foreign energy or creative energy that is stuck. Have the partners stopped creating together? Is your mother or ex in your space, preventing you from being yourself with your current love? These are possibilities to explore. Get curious and let your imagination show you answers. Perhaps some new pictures, a-has, feelings, or "out of the blue" thoughts will pop up. Using the techniques from this book plus ongoing practice, you'll begin to hone your intuitive muscles.*

• *When you're done looking at these roses, let them fly off to the edge of the horizon, and see them "pop" into bursts of light.*

• *Repeat if desired for another relationship.*

• *Before coming out of meditation, as always, fill in with a big gold sun to replenish your energy.*

HOW MUCH ARE YOU EACH INVESTING?

In a class I taught on relationships, one woman had an interesting discovery! During our meditation, we did an exercise to determine how much energy each person was putting into the relationship. Was it 50/50, or not so balanced? Some say that men "should" be putting a little more into things than they are— perhaps because they bond when they invest, because they aren't wired to bond like we are, or because we tend to over-give.

The woman in question felt that she put *way* more energy into her marriage than her husband did. She told me she made five times as much money, took personal growth classes, and received coaching. She loved him but saw him as lazy.

Then she did our meditation and saw they were even. She had an a-ha. It was taking him as much energy to do what he did as it was for her to do what she did. As a highly creative and intelligent female, her 140 watts made many things easy for her. Following that class, she softened towards him and judged him less. Magically, his career began to take off and she was able to ease off the throttle.

I have seen many, many cases like this—particularly in long-term relationships where difficult patterns have built up. One bitter side-effect of recent feminism is that it's made some women really hard on men. "I don't have to put up with that" gets taken too far, and good men get blamed just because they're not like us.

Of course, we women can certainly over-function in many of the ways named earlier in this book. Taking toxic responsibility, inappropriate mothering, and living in fantasy are some examples. If you're in a relationship and you're always leaning forward or leading the way—it's important to let him give to you more or focus your energy elsewhere if he's just not.

PRACTICE: Bringing Your Relationship into Balance

• *Sit in meditation, breathe, and ground.*

• *Next, imagine a circle, like an empty pie chart, a few feet out in front of you.*

• *Let the left side of the circle represent you and let the right side represent him. Pick a color for each of you.*

• *Now ask, "How much energy are we each putting into the relationship?" and see the pie chart fill in with your colors to answer your question. Do you see half your color and half his, or more of one or the other?*

• *Ask for any guidance about this and notice what you receive.*

• *If the energy is uneven, ground your pie chart to the center of the earth, just like you've grounded yourself.*

• *Allow the grounding cord to drain any foreign energy or blocks out of your pie chart. If there's anything keeping either of you from finding balance in the relationship, let gravity take it down into the earth.*

• *Now, like you're a kid with your magic eraser and paint, re-set the pie chart to equal parts yours and his. If you want to play with one of you giving a little more than the other, try it.*

• *Once you find the balance you like, ask for guidance: What needs to shift between you two to accomplish this? What steps can YOU take to do your part in that?*

• *When you feel complete with this practice, see the pie chart dissolve.*

• *Create a gold sun above your head and fill in with your own light.*

EMBRACING LOVE'S DANCE

A great dancer exemplifies balance in motion. Through leaps and twirls, on one foot or in the arms of a partner, she loses her balance only to find it again. Her grace is in the transitions, her beauty evident in the dynamic range of her movements. Her combination of poise and fluidity inspire awe.

Life and love are like this. Get too comfy with "balance" and it bites you in the butt. Just when you think you've embraced your Divine Feminine, life requires your masculine for a moment. And after you merge with your lover in waves of bliss, the tide must go out in order for the "pull" of union to happen again. You each need to go off and be yourselves for a moment.

We practice polarity because most of the world is shut down.

Having "all" of your masculine and "all" of your feminine means having all of your power and creative life force. Eventually, the whole point of cultivating polarity is to remember oneness. The moment your lover penetrates you, you each include the Universe. And this is where you started from.

CONCLUSION

Today's relationship models are changing, and this is exciting yet confusing for many. Gender roles and power dynamics are up for question. So much healing is occurring, and my intention is to give support to those struggling, and to inspire my fellow pioneers in creating a new way.

The good news is this: there is so much more love possible than what most of us have experienced. I am thankful to be alive at a time which allows individuals direct access to spirituality, and where people are waking up to the world of energy. The uncertainty of our times provides a creative freedom in which—assuming we stay awake-- we can't help but become our more authentic selves.

Becoming our more authentic selves means more authentic relationships. Love is who we are, and so this is a process of remembering.

This book is about living awake, as the truth of you. As you do, you can more accurately perceive energy, release what's in your way and be more present with another.

Energy is innocent. No matter what you've been through, it's something you can shift. This is simple, and it's where everything starts.

Doing the exercises in this book is like peeling the layers of the onion. You may come back to them over and over, as your life evolves. Your commitment to self-love and loving another may attract you to different practices at different times. Enjoy it all! And keep up; you are not alone.

RESOURCES

For private intuitive reading and healing sessions, upcoming events and programs along with free resources, visit www.AnnOBrienLiving. com. Or, scan the following code with your phone: